Pot Pies

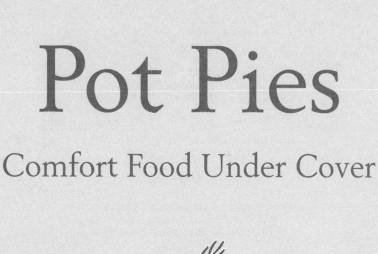

Pot Pies

Comfort Food Under Cover

Diane Phillips

DOUBLEDAY

NEW YORK LONDON TORONTO SYDNEY AUCKLAND

PUBLISHED BY DOUBLEDAY
a division of Random House, Inc.
1540 Broadway, New York, New York 10036

DOUBLEDAY and the portrayal of an anchor with a dolphin
are trademarks of Doubleday, a division of
Random House, Inc.

Design by Maggie Hinders

Library of Congress Cataloging-in-Publication Data
Phillips, Diane.
Pot pies : comfort food under cover / Diane Phillips. — 1st ed.
p.   cm.
Includes bibliographical references and index.
1. Potpies.   I. Title.
TX693.P45   2000   99-36312
641.8′24—dc21   CIP

ISBN 0-385-49458-0

Printed in the United States of America

February 2000

First Edition

1   3   5   7   9   10   8   6   4   2

To Chuck, with love.

Acknowledgments

N O ONE writes a cookbook by themselves. We stand in the kitchen with our families, friends, colleagues, and those who have inspired, encouraged, and sparked our imaginations. I was not alone while writing this book, and I would be remiss if I did not thank those who tasted, tested, and loved me through it. First a big hug to my husband Chuck, who tasted every pie. Thanks for being so patient, and not complaining when you had to eat chicken ten nights in a row. I promise you won't have to eat another crusted entree for a while! I am grateful to our children Ryan and Carrie for their enthusiastic support and for growing into such nice adults. A special thank you to my daughter Carrie, her partner Vanessa von Bismarck, and the elves at Bismarck Media Communications for providing their PR expertise and professionalism in handling "MamaD." My son Ryan's love for pot pies was the inspiration for this book, and I am thankful for his appreciation of Mom's cooking, and the joy he brings to our lives.

My agent Susan Ginsburg is always looking out for my best interests and knew where this book would have a good home. Thank you, Susan, for leaping tall buildings—your friendship is precious and I am grateful for your support and enthusiasm. Thanks also to her assistant John Hodgman, who was there at the beginning, and to Anne Stowell for taking over and having answers to all my questions.

Judy Kern, my editor at Doubleday, made this book come alive with her sharp eye for detail and organization. Thanks, Judy, for taking the ingredients and making them into a splendid feast, I consider myself fortunate to work with you. To all those at Doubleday who helped with production and promotion, I am grateful.

Special thanks to Felicia Collins and my new friends at Smith and Collins for their PR expertise, and for holding my hand during the months before publication.

My talented cousin and good friend Bill Fitz-Patrick took my photo for the book jacket; thanks, Bill, for making me laugh. I am indebted to my friend Nancy Stansbury, who came out of retirement when I called to proofread the manuscript, thanks for everything, Nancy. Lora Brody has been a source of support and encouragement, and a great e-mail buddy. Thanks, Lora, for being there when I needed a push, and when I needed a hug. To the friends and family who have supported me with their phone calls, e-mails, and offers to be crash test dummies for the recipes, please accept my gratitude as space will not allow me to thank you all individually.

Lastly I would like to thank all the cooking schools, staff, and students who have welcomed me into their kitchens over the years. A tip of the hat to Mike and Shelley Sackett at Kitchen Affairs, Loretta Paganini in Cleveland, Nancy Pigg and the Fricke family at Cookswares, Deb Lackey at Dorothy Lane Markets, Pamela Keith and the staff at Draegger's, Martha Aitken at Sur L'Table, Sandy Daniels at The Silo, Hilda Pope at Casual Gourmet, Stephen Lee at the Cookbook Cottage, and Bob Nemerovski at Ramekins. Thank you all for allowing me to come into your kitchens to do what I love.

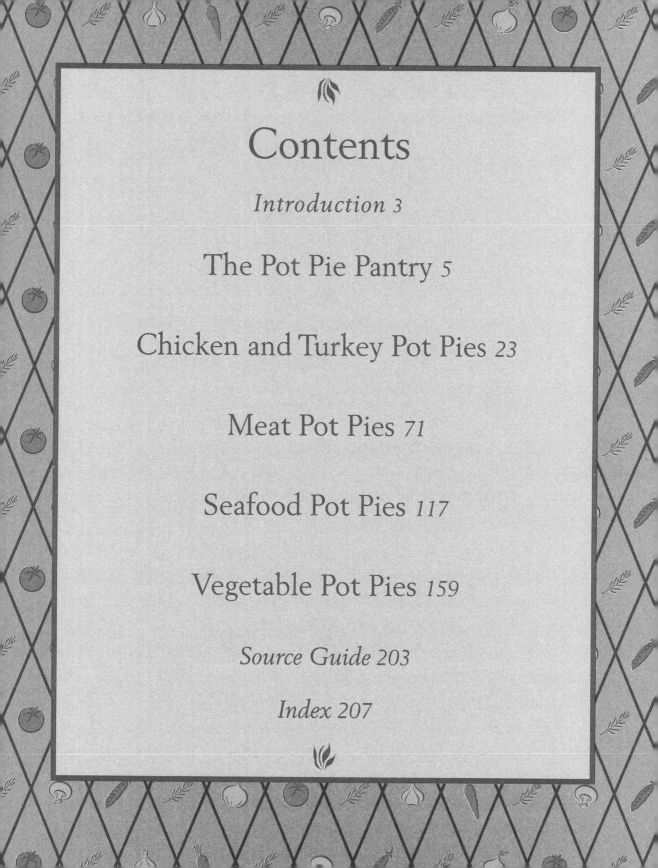

Contents

Pot Pies

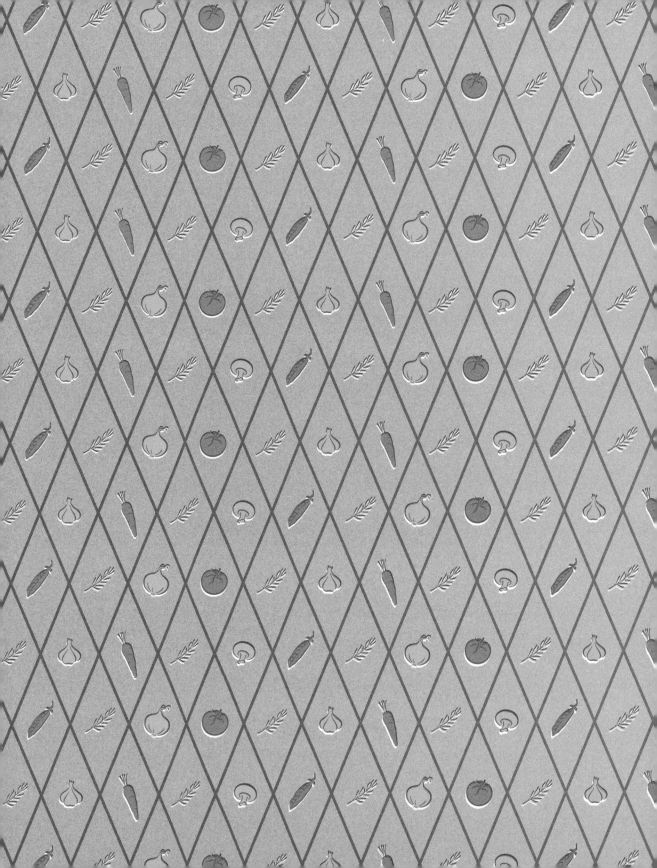

Introduction

REMEMBER coming home from school and doing your homework in the kitchen? Mom was usually there preparing dinner, and the smells from the stove soothed and relaxed you after a long day. Today you can have that same feeling of sanctuary in the kitchen by preparing comfort foods for your family. Simple, savory, and satisfying, comfort foods make home a haven and allow us to recharge after a long day.

The epitome of '50s comfort food was the pot pie: chicken or beef with vegetables in a rich sauce, topped by a flaky crust. Usually too hot to eat when it came from the oven, I'd nibble the dough edges, or my brothers would carve a hole in the center to allow the pie to cool. Once inside, the tasty reward was worth the wait. Just the fact that it had a crust, something you didn't see everyday, made it special.

Re-creating that same feeling in an era of kitchen fusion and confusion may seem like an impossible task, but where Mom made chicken and vegetables covered with pie dough, we'll cover chicken and vegetables with chive mashed potatoes. The basics are the same. Wonderful smells and savory fillings peeking out from underneath a delicious cover are the reminders we need that home is a center for peace and rest. Sitting down to a bubbling pie covered with a unique topping is what home cooking is all about. The family table can once more become a meeting place to nourish and sustain us. Mom would be proud.

A Little History

POT PIES were originally baked in a pot, over an open fire. The large pot was lined with a pastry crust, filled with meats and vegetables, topped with a crust, and then covered with the lid. A hole was made in the center of the crust, so that broth could be added from time to time. The pie would cook over the fire most of the day, perfuming the house with mouth-watering smells. Sometimes other pies were baked in wood-burning ovens, or a noodle crust was used to line the pans and cover the pies.

In 1954, the Swanson Company produced their first TV Dinners. Soon to follow the turkey and dressing dinner were turkey pot pies, made with a double crust, turkey and vegetables in a cream sauce. Swanson continues to make the turkey pot pie, but you can make your own cheaply, and in about the same amount of time it would take to bake a frozen one.

Making pot pies requires no special equipment. If you have a 13 by 9-inch baking dish, a 5-quart Dutch oven or casserole, and a 10 or 12-inch sauté pan, you can make a pot pie. Check your pantry against the list of supplies and see how well you are prepared. The fillings and toppings for most pies can be made at least two days ahead of time, giving you an advantage over the pizza delivery man. "Crusts" can be anything from a traditional pastry dough, to goat cheese mashed potatoes, to noodle pancakes, to garlic roasted red potatoes, to grilled vegetables. Toppings can also be crumbles that are strewn across the top of the filling and then baked to become a crunchy complement for the ingredients underneath. There are no hard and fast rules for the crusts, and if you like one over another with a specific dish, feel free to substitute. Using boneless cuts of meats and poultry streamlines the preparation, and shortens the cooking times.

I don't like a bottom pastry crust to my pot pies, for two reasons: one, it's more work, and two, it generally becomes soggy even with prebaking. If you decided that you absolutely can't live without a bottom crust, feel free to make one, but I recommend you prebake it.

If you love your Crock-Pot, these are a match made in heaven. Put all the filling ingredients into the Crock-Pot in the morning, then, later in the day, when you are ready to serve, cover the filling with the crust, and bake the pie.

The
Pot Pie
Pantry

The Pot Pie Pantry

T HIS pantry isn't very different from the one I recommend to my beginning cooking students. There are a few items you might not have in your pantry, such as phyllo and frozen puff pastry dough, but these can be lifesavers on a night when you really want to have some comfort food. If you have limited space, look at the items called for and decide which ones you will actually use. These will be your basics. Once you get started, you may want to add a few things you may not have tried before. After all, Mom always made you take one bite of everything, didn't she?

Spice Pantry

SPICES are your secret weapon when it comes to making meals interesting and flavorful. Check the spices you have in your pantry, and use the three-month rule: If you haven't touched, shaken, or smelled it in three months, get rid of it. Some people still have the paprika they got with their bridal shower spice rack—enough said. If there are things you have thrown away using the three-month rule, think about whether you will ever use that spice, even if it is on my list. Better to be honest and not waste your money. Store your spices in airtight jars in a cool, dry place. Don't leave them on the counter in the sun, and don't store them under a damp sink.

I recommend buying dehydrated herbs if you can find them in your supermarket; they have the closest flavor to fresh herbs. (See Source Guide.) If you cannot find dehydrated herbs, use whole dried herbs rather than ground or rubbed ones. Once the herb is ground, it loses a lot of the essential oils that make it so potent. Fresh herbs are marvelous additions to any dish, but I don't recommend them for dishes that will simmer longer than 30 minutes—the herbs break down and lose most of their flavor when cooked for a long time. To store fresh herbs, I recommend washing them in cold water and thoroughly drying them in a salad spinner or with dry towels. Store them in Ziploc bags with a dry paper towel to absorb the moisture, or fill a small jar with water and "plant" the herbs in the water. If you have lots of fresh parsley, chop it in the food processor and store it in Ziploc bags in the freezer—use it right from the bag.

HERBS

BASIL	ROSEMARY
BAY LEAVES	SAGE
DILLWEED	TARRAGON
MARJORAM	THYME
OREGANO	

SPICES

BLACK PEPPERCORNS	MUSTARD (DRY POWDER)
CAYENNE	NUTMEG (WHOLE)
CHILI POWDER	OLD BAY SEASONING
CINNAMON	POPPY SEEDS
CUMIN	SAFFRON
CURRY POWDER	SESAME SEEDS
GINGER (GROUND)	

Creole Seasoning

Creole Seasoning is an essential in my pantry. I make it up myself, using this recipe, but you can certainly purchase it at the supermarket. I like to make up a batch, then give small jars of it to friends.

$^1/_4$ cup onion powder

$^1/_4$ cup dried thyme

$^1/_4$ cup freshly ground black pepper

$^1/_2$ cup garlic powder

$^1/_2$ cup salt

$^1/_2$ cup paprika

$^1/_4$ cup cayenne

2 tablespoons dried oregano

In a glass bowl, combine all the ingredients, whisking to blend. Store in an airtight container for up to 3 months.

Yield is about 2 $^1/_2$ cups.

Refrigerator and Freezer

THE following list assumes that you have the essentials in your refrigerator already: milk, butter (or margarine), eggs, juice, and chocolate chip cookie dough ice cream.

Bread Crumbs

Fresh and dry bread crumbs can be stored in the freezer indefinitely, and they can be used to enhance pot pie crusts. When that baguette from the patisserie gets too hard, place it in a self-seal bag and run a rolling pin over it for bread crumbs. Store it in the freezer.

Capers

Small in size, big on flavor, this cousin of the green peppercorn can make chicken or veal into a deliciously different dinner.

Cheese

Everyone has their favorite types of cheese. I love Cabot Farms White Cheddar, Gruyère, Monterey Jack, and Brie. Pick your favorite, and store it in the refrigerator for everything from quesadillas to Cheddar cheese crusts.

Chicken

I buy fresh boneless, skinless chicken breasts and freeze them in packages of 4. If you have a larger family, you may want to freeze more in each package. Boneless breasts can be used for quick dinners any time.

Frozen Shrimp

Peeled and deveined raw shrimp are a quick and easy way to turn any meal into something special.

Frozen Vegetables

I always have corn, petite size peas, and chopped spinach in my freezer. These vegetables can be used to make almost any dinner special.

Granny Smith Apples

Tart, and crunchy, these are great for eating, but they also make delicious pies and can go into pork and chicken dishes as well.

Lemons

Fresh lemon juice and zest add zip to many dishes. Don't buy the little plastic lemon in the supermarket, it's really awful.

Packaged Salad Greens

Always appropriate, a nice simple salad is like wearing pearls—it's never out of style and pairs well with any pot pie! Bags of baby spinach are great for making piecrusts too.

Parmesan Cheese

There is nothing more sublime, in my humble opinion, than slivers of Parmigiano-Reggiano cheese. Keeping a small wedge of Parmigiano-Reggiano in your fridge will help to perk up ordinary ingredients. To store the cheese, dampen a paper towel with some olive oil, wrap the cheese in the paper, and store it in a self-seal bag. I also keep some grated Parmesan in small quantities to toss into pastas and other dishes.

Pesto in a Tube

Prepared pesto can add pizzazz to sauces and crusts for your pies. The tube keeps a long time in the fridge.

Phyllo Dough

Mostly sold in the freezer section, phyllo keeps for up to 6 months, and makes a buttery, flaky topping for any pie.

Puff Pastry Sheets

Frozen, these sheets defrost in 20 minutes on the counter and roll out to become delicious crusts for any pie.

Sour Cream

Sour cream makes a rich addition to sauces and a nice accompaniment for pot pies.

Tortillas

Flour or corn, these wrappers can be used as crusts or to layer between ingredients in pies. Refrigerate or freeze them.

Dry Pantry

THIS list assumes that you have the essentials in your dry pantry, such as flour, corn-meal, Bisquick, sugar, brown sugar, leavenings (yeast, baking powder, and soda), and chocolate chips.

Artichoke Hearts
Canned artichoke hearts are great to use in a pinch. They can be paired with other vegetables and made into wonderful vegetarian pies, or they can become a crust for seafood or chicken.

Canned Beans
Keep an assortment of canned beans on hand to enhance your pies and to use as crusts. Beans help to stretch your meat and are an excellent source of fiber and protein.

Canned Chopped Tomatoes
When fresh tomatoes are looking sad in the supermarket, feel free to use canned chopped tomatoes in any of your recipes. These are great to keep in your pantry for a quick pasta sauce, soup, or stew.

Canned Stock
Canned stock can help to make a very nice pot pie. Try different brands of stock, and decide which one you like best. Also, there are several soup bases on the market that reconstitute with water and tend to be a bit more economical.

Many gourmet grocers sell their own stock "concentrate" as well, but it tends to be a bit pricey. If you have the time to make your own stock, follow the instructions on pages 20–22. Store the finished stock in the refrigerator or freezer.

Dijon Mustard
Dijon mustard adds pizzazz to many dishes and can also be used to make a killer ham sandwich.

Dried Pastas
Dried pastas are great to keep in your pantry for those days when you need a quick-fix for dinner. Try to keep several different shapes on hand.

Fresh Garlic

There is nothing better than the mellow flavor of garlic. Don't substitute granulated garlic for fresh garlic in your recipes; the flavor will not be nearly as good. I don't recommend buying the chopped garlic that is preserved in small jars, it tends to have an "off" taste.

Fresh Ginger

A knob of ginger, peeled, sliced, and put into some sherry, will keep in the refrigerator for months. To store the fresh ginger unpeeled, keep it in a cool, dry spice cabinet.

Non-Stick Cooking Spray

Hate to clean baking dishes and cookie sheets? Keep a can of non-stick cooking spray in your pantry to spray on your baking dishes and keep your pies from sticking. You can also buy one of those new pump-type sprayers, and fill it with your own oil.

Olive Oil

If you can afford the space, buy a small bottle of good extra virgin olive oil and another of a lighter variety. For everyday cooking, use the lighter olive oil (I like Bertoli), but for a more robust taste, use the extra virgin. I find the extra virgin can overpower many foods, so use it sparingly.

Onions

I keep red onions in my basket all year, for salads and sometimes for cooking. I buy sweet yellow onions, and keep them as well. In the winter, yellow onions tend to be very strong, so spend the extra money and buy sweet Maui, Texas, or Vidalia sweet onions. You will be happy with the results.

Orzo

Orzo is a rice-shaped pasta that makes a great crust for pot pies, as well as being an interesting side dish on its own.

Oyster Sauce

Found in the Asian section of the supermarket or in Asian markets, it's a great flavoring to have on the shelf. Refrigerate it after opening.

Potatoes

Baking or russet potatoes and new potatoes (I prefer the red variety) can be used for mashing, boiling, or sautéing. Russets make great potato pancakes and mashed potatoes, and red potatoes are wonderful roasted.

Rice

Rice can be stored for a long time in airtight containers. If you have the space, try keeping some wild rice and basmati rice on hand, too.

Sesame Oil

Made from toasted sesame seeds, this oil adds an exotic flavor to many dishes. After opening, make sure to refrigerate it.

Shallots

A member of the onion family, shallots pack a lot of flavor into a small bulb.

Sherry

Sherry adds a nutty flavor to any dish. Keep a bottle in the pantry.

Shortening

Vegetable shortening such as Crisco makes flaky biscuits and can be used in piecrust doughs as well.

Soy Sauce

An imported soy sauce will add Asian flavor and salt to your dishes.

Sun-dried Tomatoes

I like to buy sun-dried tomatoes packed in olive oil. You can use the oil for flavoring and the tomatoes are a colorful addition to any dish.

Tabasco Sauce

Everyone needs a little heat in their dishes, and Tabasco is still the most reliable for flavor and heat. If you have a favorite hot sauce, feel free to substitute it. Once opened, you should refrigerate the sauce.

Tomato paste in Tubes

I bless the person who invented tomato paste in a tube. This product replaces tiny cans that are hard to open and always contain more than you need. It stores in the refrigerator after opening, keeps for 12 months, and you can use as much or as little as you need.

Vermouth

Dry vermouth keeps well, and can be used instead of white wine in cooking.

Vegetable Oil

For sautéing, find an oil that you like. I generally use Canola oil, but you can use corn, or a combination of corn and Canola.

Worcestershire Sauce

A flavoring no kitchen should be without, Worcestershire livens up seafood and chicken as well as beef.

Gadgets

FORTUNATELY, making pot pies will not require you to go out and invest in any new gadgets. The good news is, you can dust off that ten-inch Pyrex pie pan you've got hidden and you can use all those great Corning casseroles that you got for your wedding shower. Now, if you think you deserve something new, invest in a heavy 5-quart Dutch oven. There are lots of pretty ones on the market, from cast iron with enameled porcelain in a variety of colors, to beautifully decorated pottery. The sky is the limit. There are some things I can't live without, and I've given you that list below.

Crock-Pot

Crock-Pots are great for working people. Just throw the ingredients into the pot and let her rip. Six hours later you have perfect stews and fillings for pot pies. Just make the crust and bake.

Cutting Boards

I use plastic cutting boards because they can be washed in the dishwasher. Wooden boards are gorgeous, but they are high maintenance and I'm not into that. I have 4 different sizes of cutting boards, and love to use them.

Food Processor

This is my desert island piece of equipment. If I were marooned on a desert island, I would want this (and a portable generator), so that I could knead bread doughs; make piecrusts; grate cheese; make pesto, hollandaise, and all manner of sauces; as well as slice and dice all the tropical fruits and vegetables I would gather. An essential (in my humble opinion), this wonder machine has revolutionized the twentieth-century kitchen.

Mixer

You may not have room for a heavy-duty standing mixer, but do get yourself something that can whip cream, mash potatoes, or mix bread doughs. It will take some of the hard work out of these jobs.

Sharp Knives

Sharp knives just make chopping and slicing so much easier. Invest in knives that feel right in your hand. Some people buy chef's knives that only a burly sumo wrestler could wield, and then say, "I hate these knives," without having tried anything else.

If you have a set of knives that you like, but if they are dull, take them to a professional sharpener. All knives need to be professionally sharpened even though the manufacturers of "at home" sharpeners would tell you otherwise. As basics, I recommend a paring knife, a chef's knife or cleaver (to fit your hand), and a serrated knife. Once you are comfortable with those, you can buy a carving knife, boning knife, and whatever else you need.

Spatulas
Okay, I know you have some of these, but do you have the new, heat-tempered ones that can withstand up to 400° F.? You can use them for stirring sauces without fear of their melting into something that looks like ET.

Whisks
Invest in a whisk to help make your sauces smooth. To start with, I would get one 10-inch sauce whisk and one balloon whisk.

13 by 9-Inch Casserole
When I got married, someone gave me a 13 by 9-inch casserole dish, and I still have it. Made of plain tempered Pyrex glass, it's not stylish, but it sure serves a purpose. From baking large pot pies to delicious cakes and cobblers, I use it all the time. And for special occasions, I have several others that are painted, ovenproof porcelain.

The Basics

UNLESS otherwise stated on the recipe ingredients list, the following rules apply:

Eggs
Use the large size.

Garlic
Usually a medium garlic clove is needed, not from a super-large head.

Onion
This means one medium yellow onion; yields about 1 cup chopped or sliced.

Fat
In general, I use butter rather than margarine because I prefer the taste, but you can certainly substitute margarine for butter in all these recipes. If you would like to use a lower fat cheese, use low-fat rather than non-fat. Non-fat cheeses have little flavor and melt like wax. Feel free to substitute non-fat yogurt for sour cream, and where there is a sauce enhanced by heavy cream, you may omit the heavy cream and substitute more broth. The resulting pie will probably not be as rich, but you will have saved a few fat grams, if that is important to you.

Milk and Heavy Cream
All of the recipes were tested using whole milk and 2 percent milk. While whole milk and heavy cream gave a richer sauce, the 2 percent milk worked just fine. I don't recommend using skim milk for these recipes, as the sauce just isn't the same. Where heavy cream is called for, I think it makes a difference, but you should feel free to use whole milk or 2 percent if you prefer. The sauce will not be as rich, but you've been warned!

Getting Started

Browning

Browning the meat in a hot pan before it goes into the sauce seals in the juices, as well as helping to enrich the flavor and color of the sauce. I highly recommend that you brown the meats before adding the liquids. If you decide to make any of these fillings in a Crock-Pot, try to brown the meat first, since it will make a difference in the taste of the finished dish.

Herbs

Fresh or dried, whole or rubbed—which is best? If you are simmering something for over 30 minutes, use a whole dried herb. Rubbed or crushed herbs lose some of their essential oils, and are not as flavorful. Fresh herbs are so delicate in flavor that if you simmer them longer than 30 minutes they will lose any flavor they had. A dried whole herb will stand up to long simmering and add the proper balance of flavor. At the end of the cooking time, stir in some fresh herbs to refresh the flavor of the sauce. I like to use dehydrated herbs, which are sold in the supermarkets. (See Source Guide.)

Salt and Pepper

I keep an open dish of sea salt and a pepper grinder loaded with whole black peppercorns by my stove. Salt brings out the natural flavors and juices in foods, and I recommend that you season your foods at the beginning, in the middle, and again at the end. Since salt is a matter of individual taste, I have given you a place to start for a balanced dish. Freshly ground pepper also spikes up the flavor, so give yourself a gift and invest in a nice pepper grinder. You won't be sorry.

Serving Sizes

Most of the recipes in this book will serve 6 to 8. That means that 6 people with normal appetites will have 2 portions left over for another meal, or a second helping, and 8 people will have nothing left over. Since portion size is a matter of individual taste, I have given you a range. This also allows you to double the recipes for a larger group. If the recipe calls for individual portions of meat, as in the Beef Fillets with Wild Mushrooms and Maytag Blue Cheese, there is 1 portion of beef for each person. I find after years of catering and serving to people that if the meat or poultry is cut up, people generally eat half the amount they would eat if it were a whole portion (as in a chicken breast). The good news is that these pot pies will save you money, and you can stretch the protein with the addition of veggies and carbohydrates.

Stock

In a perfect world, we would make our own chicken or beef stock, and I have included recipes to accomplish this. Since it isn't a perfect world, you can substitute your favorite commercial brand of broth. There are many brands on the market, with varying degrees of sodium and fat to choose from. There are also soup bases (see Source Guide) and concentrates you can buy and reconstitute with water. If you buy a soup base, make sure the first ingredient on the list is chicken if it's a chicken base, or beef if it's a beef base.

How to Make Homemade Stocks

*M*aking homemade stock is something that can be done on a weekend afternoon when you have a little bit of time. Stock is not complicated, but it does take time and some attention. Once you have made the stock, you will have a nice treasure in your freezer to tap into when you want to make a special soup for your family.

Chicken Stock

2 whole chickens, quartered, about 3 pounds each

2 medium onions, quartered

3 stalks celery, chopped into 4 pieces each

2 carrots, cut into 4 pieces each

1 teaspoon dried thyme

2 teaspoons salt

4 sprigs fresh parsley

4 whole black peppercorns

8 cups water

In an 8-quart stockpot, combine all the ingredients. Bring the water to a boil and reduce the heat to a simmer. Skim the foam that forms on top of the water, and simmer the soup uncovered for 1½ hours. Remove the large pieces of meat and vegetables from the soup and strain the stock into a glass bowl. Remove the chicken from the bones and refrigerate it for another use. Store the stock in the refrigerator until the fat solidifies on the top. Remove the fat, and refrigerate the stock for up to 4 days, or freeze it for 2 months.

Makes about 5 cups

Beef Stock

5 pounds beef bones

5 cloves garlic

4 medium onions, quartered

4 large carrots, cut into 4 pieces each

4 medium stalks celery, cut into 4 pieces each

8 cups water

2 teaspoons salt

4 whole black peppercorns

Preheat the oven to 425° F. Place the bones and garlic in the bottom of a large roasting pan. Roast the bones for 1 hour, turning them after 30 minutes. Add the vegetables to the roasting pan, and roast for another 20 minutes.

Transfer the bones and vegetables to an 8- to 10-quart stockpot. Remove the fat from the roasting pan, and pour the water into the pan. Scrape up any browned bits from the bottom of the pan and add the contents of the roasting pan to the pot. Add the salt and pepper, and bring to a boil over high heat. Reduce the heat to a simmer, and cook, uncovered, for 1½ hours. Remove the bones from the soup and strain the stock. Discard all the vegetables and bones. Return the stock to the pot and simmer, uncovered, for another hour. Refrigerate the stock until the fat has solidified. Remove the fat from the top and refrigerate the stock for 4 days, or freeze it for up to 2 months.

Makes 2 quarts

Turkey Carcass Soup

1 turkey carcass, cut into 3 or 4 pieces

2 large onions, quartered

3 carrots, coarsely chopped

3 stalks celery, coarsely chopped

$1/2$ teaspoon dried thyme

$1/2$ teaspoon dried sage

5 whole black peppercorns

8 cups water

Any leftover turkey dressing or gravy

Place all the ingredients into a large stockpot. Cover the pot and bring the liquid to a boil. Reduce the heat to a simmer, skimming off any foam that may have accumulated on the top. Simmer the soup, uncovered, for at least 4 hours, stirring occasionally to break up the bones. Cool the soup, straining the vegetables and meat from the broth. Save any large pieces of meat for salad, sandwiches, or casseroles. Refrigerate the broth and skim the fat from the top. Store in the freezer for up to 3 months.

Makes 2 to 3 quarts

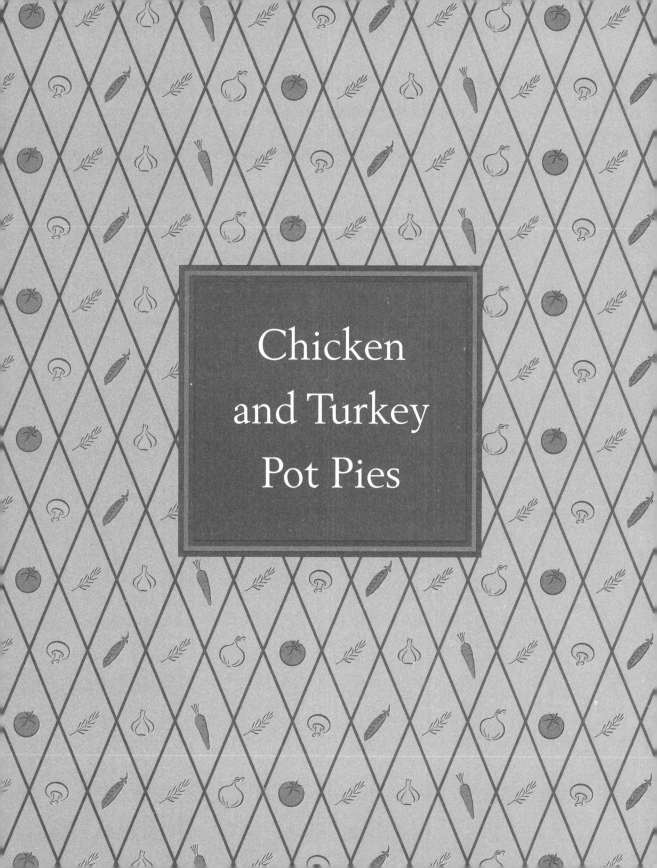

Chicken and Turkey Pot Pies

Chicken Bouillabaisse with Rouille Crust

Chicken Gumbo Pie with Buttermilk Biscuit Crust

Chicken Monterey with Corn Chile Cheese Topping

Chicken Spinach Cannelloni Pie

Chicken with Eggplant Gorgonzola Crust

Chicken with Ratatouille Brie Crust

Coq au Vin au Crouton

Lemon Herbed Chicken with Grilled Vegetable Topping

Lone Star Chicken Chili Topped with Refried Bean Crust

Ryan's Pie

Tuscan Chicken Topped with Roasted Red Potato Crust

Moroccan Chicken Pie

Not Your Mother's Chicken Divan

Old-Fashioned Chicken Pot Pie with Chive
Mashed Potato Crust

Oriental Chicken and Vegetables Topped
with Noodle Pancake

Turkey Cassoulet with Puree of White Beans, Garlic,
Parmesan, and Parsley Crust

Turkey Meat Loaf Surprise

Turkey Orlof with Creamy Onion Rice Topping

Turkey Pie with Cranberry Thyme Crust

Turkey Pot Pie with Onion Sage Dressing

Turkey Squash Pie with White Cheddar and Bacon Crust

Turkey Vegetable Dill Pie with Chive Biscuit Crust

Monte Cristo Pie

Our love affair with chicken and turkey knows no bounds. They used to be reserved for Sunday dinner, where we would sit down at a table laden with vegetables, and a roasted bird as the centerpiece of the meal. Dad would carve, and it was a special occasion. When Sunday dinners gave way to football games on television, we were making Buffalo wings and barbecued chicken for munching while watching the game. When alarmists were decrying the dangers of red meat, chicken consumption skyrocketed, except that it was served dry and unadorned. What happened to Mom's roast chicken, and what happened to comfort food? Losing sight of the fact that it should taste good, some of us were serving chicken with little flavor, until our families were complaining.

Well, it's time to liven up that poultry by covering it with great crusts. Poultry is so versatile because it adapts well to lots of different cooking techniques and seasonings. Roasting, braising, stir-frying, baking, and grilling all show off poultry at its best. By using crusts, you'll be able to seal in the natural juices of the poultry and enhance its flavor, so that it will taste like chicken used to taste.

Poultry pies are great vehicles to recycle leftovers. A few cups of leftover chicken or turkey combined with vegetables and sauce, crusted with potatoes, pasta, or biscuits, can make a weeknight dinner into a special occasion. Boneless cuts of chicken or turkey can be found at the supermarket and make the best choices for pot pies, eliminating the necessity for boning the meat before it goes into the pie. Low in fat and easy to prepare, chicken is on most family tables at least two nights a week. If you are buying a rotisserie chicken one night, turn the leftovers into a pot pie the next. The flavor will be completely different from the previous meal.

Chicken Bouillabaisse with Rouille Crust

*B*ouillabaisse, that saffron-scented seafood soup, gets a new spin with chicken and rice. *The crust is a take-off on rouille, a classic French garlic sauce, but here it is spread on croutons and baked until golden. The bouillabaisse is actually better if it sits overnight before serving.*

BOUILLABAISSE FILLING
8 skinless and boneless chicken thighs

1 teaspoon salt

1/2 teaspoon cayenne

2 tablespoons olive oil

1 large onion, sliced 1/2 inch thick

3 cloves garlic, minced

1/8 teaspoon saffron, crumbled

1 cup white wine

1 (15 1/2-ounce) can chopped tomatoes

2 1/2 cups chicken broth

1 teaspoon fresh thyme, or 1/2 teaspoon dried

1/2 cup long-grain rice

1 recipe Rouille Crust (see below)

12 slices French bread, cut 3/4 inch thick, toasted on both sides

To make the filling, sprinkle the chicken with the salt and cayenne. Heat the oil in a 5-quart Dutch oven, add the chicken, and brown it on all sides. Remove the chicken to a plate and add the onion to the pot, stirring until the onion is softened. Add the garlic and saffron, stirring for 1 minute. Pour in the wine and bring it to a boil, stirring up any browned bits that may have accumulated on the bottom of the pan. Add the tomatoes, chicken broth, and thyme, stirring to blend. Return the chicken to the pan, lower the heat and simmer, uncovered, for 25 minutes. Add the rice and cook for 15 minutes more. (The bouillabaisse may be refrigerated at this point for 2 days.)

Make the rouille.

Preheat the oven to 375° F. Heat the bouillabaisse to serving temperature. Spread 1 to 2 tablespoons of rouille onto each piece of toast, and float the bread on top of the bouillabaisse, cutting the bread to fit in one layer. Bake the pie in the preheated oven for 20 minutes, until the rouille is bubbling. Remove from the oven and serve immediately.

Rouille Crust

This garlicky red pepper sauce is like pesto in its preparation, and can be stored in the refrigerator for 7 days, or frozen for 2 months. If you don't have extra virgin olive oil, use 3/4 cup regular olive oil.

2 roasted red bell peppers (either fresh, page 185, or jarred)

4 cloves garlic

1/2 teaspoon salt

1/4 teaspoon freshly ground black pepper

1 cup fresh basil leaves, loosely packed

6 shakes Tabasco sauce

1/2 cup fresh French bread crumbs

1/4 cup extra virgin olive oil

1/2 cup olive oil

Place the red peppers, garlic, salt, black pepper, basil, Tabasco, and bread crumbs in the work bowl of a food processor fitted with a metal blade. Pulse the mixture on and off 3 times. With the machine running, add the oil slowly through the feed tube, processing, until smooth. Remove the sauce from the work bowl and store it in the refrigerator.

Serves 6 to 8

Chicken Gumbo Pie with Buttermilk Biscuit Crust

*G*umbo is one of those dishes that takes its flavors from the cook's whim. This gumbo with chicken and spicy sausage can be made ahead, and the buttermilk biscuit crust will become one of your favorites. Cooking a roux is not difficult, but don't try doing it when you are going to be distracted, as you will need to stir it constantly.

GUMBO FILLING
1/2 cup vegetable oil

1/2 cup flour

1 1/2 cups chopped onion

1 1/2 cups chopped green bell pepper

1 1/2 cups chopped celery

6 cloves garlic, mashed

1 tablespoon Creole Seasoning (page 8)

4 cups cooked chicken cut into 1/2-inch pieces

1 pound andouille or Polish sausage cut into 1/2-inch rounds

6 cups chicken stock

1 recipe Buttermilk Biscuit Crust (see below)

2 tablespoons melted butter

In a 5-quart Dutch oven over medium heat, heat the oil. Add the flour and cook, stirring until the flour is the color of light caramels. This should take about 5 minutes. Add the onion, pepper, celery, garlic, and Creole seasoning, stirring and cooking for another 5 minutes. Add the chicken and sausage and cook for three minutes. Gradually add the chicken stock to the pot, whisking until the sauce is thickened. Reduce the heat to a simmer and cook, partially covered, for 30 minutes. Refrigerate the filling for up to two days before baking. Reheat to serving temperature before baking.

Make the crust. When ready to bake with the crust, transfer the filling to an ovenproof baking and serving dish. Preheat the oven to 425° F. Brush the biscuits with the melted butter, and bake the pot pie for 15 to 20 minutes, until it's golden.

Buttermilk Biscuit Crust

2 cups all-purpose flour

1 tablespoon baking powder

$^1/_2$ teaspoon baking soda

$^1/_2$ teaspoon salt

6 tablespoons vegetable shortening

$^3/_4$ cup buttermilk

In a large mixing bowl, whisk together the flour, baking powder, baking soda, and salt. Cut in the shortening, and stir in the buttermilk until the dough begins to form. Turn the dough out onto a lightly floured board and roll it out $^1/_2$-inch thick. Cut out individual biscuits and lay them on top of the gumbo.

Serves 8

Chicken Monterey with Corn Chile Cheese Topping

*C*hicken rolls stuffed with green chilies and Monterey Jack cheese are covered with a creamy corn, tortilla, and Colby cheese crust for an unusual pie with a Southwestern accent. Serve this with an orange and avocado salad, and rice.

8 skinless and boneless chicken breast halves

1 teaspoon salt

1/2 teaspoon freshly ground black pepper

1/2 cup finely chopped roasted green chilies

1 cup grated Monterey Jack cheese

2 tablespoons butter

2 cups fresh, or frozen and defrosted corn kernels

2 cups corn tortillas, torn into 1-inch pieces

1/2 cup milk

2 tablespoons chopped fresh cilantro, plus additional for garnish

2 tablespoons fresh tomato salsa (page 172)

1 cup grated Colby cheese

Sour cream, for garnish

Preheat the oven to 350° F. Place each chicken breast between 2 pieces of waxed paper and pound them flat with the base of a wine bottle, a rolling pin, or a meat tenderizer. Season the pounded breasts with the salt and pepper.

In a small bowl, combine the chilies and Monterey Jack cheese. Divide the mixture evenly among the chicken breasts, placing the stuffing in the center of each breast. Fold one end of the chicken over the filling, fold in the sides, and roll the chicken into a neat package. Refrigerate the rolls for 2 hours, or until ready to bake.

In a sauté pan, melt the butter and sauté the chicken rolls until they are lightly browned on all sides, about 5 minutes. Remove them to a baking dish that will hold them comfortably in one layer. (A 10-inch round pie plate works well.) In the work bowl of a food processor, combine 1 cup of the corn with the tortillas, milk, and cilantro. Process until the corn is creamy and the tortillas are combined with the milk. Remove to a mixing bowl and fold in the remaining corn and the tomato salsa. (Refrigerate until ready to bake.) Pour the crust over the chicken and sprinkle it with the grated Colby cheese. Bake the pie for 35 to 45 minutes, until the top is golden brown. Serve garnished with sour cream and additional chopped cilantro.

Serves 6 to 8

Chicken Spinach Cannelloni Pie

I love cannelloni, but I hate taking the time to fill the tubes of pasta. This recipe makes my favorite chicken and spinach filling into a delicious noodle-crusted pie covered with a cheesy garlic white sauce that's striped with tomato sauce. If you can get fresh pasta noodles, do not boil them before baking; otherwise, cook regular lasagna noodles according to the manufacturer's directions. If you would like to substitute cooked fish or shellfish for the chicken, it works very well in this recipe.

CHICKEN AND SPINACH FILLING

2 cups cooked chopped spinach (1$\frac{1}{2}$ pounds steamed, or one 10-ounce packaged
frozen chopped spinach, defrosted and squeezed dry)

2 cups cooked cubed chicken or turkey

$\frac{1}{4}$ cup chopped fresh flat-leaf parsley

3 large eggs

2 cups ricotta cheese

$\frac{3}{4}$ cup freshly grated Parmesan cheese

1 teaspoon salt

$\frac{1}{2}$ teaspoon freshly ground black pepper

1 recipe Tomato Sauce (see below)

1 recipe Parmesan Garlic Sauce (page 36)

3 sheets fresh pasta to fit a 13 by 9-inch ovenproof baking dish, or $\frac{3}{4}$ pound dry
lasagna noodles, cooked and drained

In a large mixing bowl, combine the spinach, chicken, and parsley. In another bowl, beat together the eggs, ricotta, $\frac{1}{2}$ cup Parmesan, salt, and pepper. Add the chicken and spinach to the bowl, and stir to combine. Refrigerate for up to 8 hours before assembling the cannelloni.

Preheat the oven to 350 degrees. Spray a 13 by 9-inch ovenproof baking dish with non-stick oil spray. Spoon $1/2$ cup of tomato sauce into the bottom of the baking dish. Cover the sauce with one of the lasagna noodles. Spread half of the cannelloni filling over the noodles. Cover with another layer of noodles. Spread half of the Parmesan garlic sauce over the noodles, and stripe the white sauce with $1/2$ cup of the tomato sauce. Cover with the remaining cannelloni filling. Top with the remaining lasagna noodles. Cover with the remaining Parmesan sauce, and top with the remaining tomato sauce. Sprinkle with the remaining Parmesan cheese, and bake the pie for 45 minutes, until the cheese is golden and the pie is bubbling. Let the pie rest for 10 minutes before serving.

Tomato Sauce

2 tablespoons olive oil

1 cup chopped onion

6 cups peeled, seeded, and chopped tomatoes or 3 ($15^1/2$-ounce) cans

$1^1/2$ teaspoons salt

$1/2$ teaspoon freshly ground black pepper

1 tablespoon sugar

2 tablespoons chopped fresh basil

$1/4$ cup chopped fresh Italian flat-leaf parsley

In a 4-quart saucepan, heat the oil and sauté the onion for 3 minutes. Add the tomatoes, salt, pepper, sugar, and basil and simmer the sauce, uncovered, for 30 minutes. Stir in the parsley and cook for an additional 10 minutes. Taste for seasoning, and correct with additional salt and pepper if desired. The sauce may be refrigerated for 2 days, or frozen for 2 months.

recipe continues on following page

continued from previous page

Parmesan Garlic Sauce

*This is one of those all-purpose sauces to which you can add chicken,
vegetables, or fish, then toss with pasta and serve as a main course.*

6 tablespoons butter
1 clove garlic, mashed
6 tablespoons all-purpose four
3 cups milk
$1/2$ teaspoon salt
6 shakes Tabasco sauce
Pinch of grated nutmeg
$1/2$ cup freshly grated Parmesan cheese

In a 3-quart saucepan, melt the butter, add the garlic, and sauté for 1 minute to soften the garlic. Add the flour and whisk until smooth. Allow the flour to bubble, then add the milk slowly, whisking until the sauce is smooth and thick. Add the salt, Tabasco, nutmeg, and cheese. Whisk until the cheese is melted. Taste and correct the seasoning if necessary. Refrigerate the sauce until ready to finish the pie.

Serves 6 to 8

Chicken with Eggplant Gorgonzola Crust

A local caterer where I live charges a huge fee for this deliciously easy and eye-appealing main course. Now you can make it at home, and take the bows. The entire dish can be made ahead, with a brief warm-up in the oven.

8 skinless and boneless chicken breast halves

2 teaspoons salt

2 teaspoons freshly ground black pepper

1 tablespoon butter

3 to 4 tablespoons olive oil

2 tablespoons port wine (optional)

1 large eggplant (about 1½ pounds), cut into ½-inch-thick rounds

½ pound crumbled Gorgonzola cheese

Preheat the oven to 400° F. Place each chicken breast between 2 sheets of waxed paper and pound them flat with a rolling pin or meat tenderizer. Sprinkle the flattened chicken breasts with 1 teaspoon of the salt and ½ teaspoon of the pepper. In a 12-inch sauté pan, heat the butter and 1 tablespoon of the oil. Sauté the chicken until it is lightly browned on both sides, 3 minutes a side. Transfer the chicken to a 13 by 9-inch ovenproof baking dish. Deglaze the sauté pan with the port, if desired, and, when the mixture is reduced, pour it over the chicken. (Refrigerate until ready to bake.)

Heat 1 tablespoon of olive oil in the same sauté pan. Add the eggplant, a few slices at a time, seasoning it with the additional salt and pepper. Add more oil if needed. Sauté until the eggplant is softened. Eggplant softens after 2 minutes on each side. It doesn't brown. Add more oil as necessary. Top the chicken with the cooked eggplant. (At this point, the dish may be covered with plastic wrap and refrigerated for up to 2 days.) Sprinkle the Gorgonzola over the eggplant and bake the pie for 15 minutes, until the cheese is melted. Serve immediately.

Serves 6 to 8

Chicken with Ratatouille Brie Crust

*M*y family used to complain about how boring chicken was until they tasted this eye-appealing pie. As sautéed chicken breasts bake under spicy ratatouille covered with mellow slivers of Brie, they become juicy and succulent. There are many recipes for ratatouille, and you should feel free to add to or subtract from the vegetables called for in this recipe. Eggplant is always used, but the amounts of zucchini and peppers can be tailored to your family's taste.

2 tablespoons extra virgin olive oil

8 skinless and boneless chicken breast halves

3 teaspoons salt

1 1/2 teaspoons freshly ground black pepper

2 large onions, sliced into 1/2-inch pieces (about 2 cups)

2 cloves garlic, minced

1 small eggplant (about 1/2 pound), sliced into 1/2-inch rounds

1 green bell pepper, sliced into 1/2-inch pieces

1 red bell pepper, sliced into 1/2-inch pieces

4 small zucchini, sliced into 1/4-inch rounds

1/2 teaspoon dried marjoram

1/2 teaspoon dried thyme

1/2 teaspoon dried oregano

1 1/2 cups peeled, seeded, and chopped tomatoes

2 tablespoons chopped fresh flat-leaf parsley

1/2 to 3/4 pound Brie cheese, rind removed, sliced 1/2 inch thick

Preheat the oven to 400° F. In a 12-inch sauté pan, heat 1 tablespoon of the olive oil. Season the chicken with 1 teaspoon of the salt and 1/2 teaspoon of the pepper, and sauté the breasts until they are lightly browned, 3–4 minutes on each side. Transfer the chicken to a 13 by 9-inch ovenproof dish. Refrigerate until ready to use. In the same sauté pan, heat the remaining 1 tablespoon of oil, add the onions and garlic, and sauté for 2 minutes over high heat, taking care not to burn the garlic. Add the eggplant, sautéing and stirring for 2 minutes, then add the green and red peppers and the zucchini, and season with the remaining salt and pepper, then marjoram, thyme, and oregano. Toss and sauté the vegetables for 5 minutes, until they begin to soften. Add the tomatoes and continue to sauté for another 5 minutes, until the tomatoes give off some of their juices. Stir in the parsley, taste for seasoning, and spread the ratatouille over the chicken breasts in the pan. Cover with the Brie. The Brie may just come off in clumps, but that's okay, because it will melt in the oven. Bake the pie for 15 minutes, until the Brie is melted. Serve with hot, crusty French bread.

Serves 6 to 8

Coq au Vin au Crouton

*T*his pie combines 2 of my favorite dishes, a classic chicken in red wine sauce and French onion soup. The chicken can be made several days ahead of time and stored in the refrigerator. Warmed up in the oven to heat through and melt the cheesy crouton topping, it's perfect for a quick last-minute dinner.

2 tablespoons butter

6 small onions (1^{1}/2 inches in diameter), quartered

1 pound small white mushrooms, cleaned

3 cloves garlic, minced

3 pounds boneless chicken thighs and half breasts (4 of each would be nice)

1 teaspoon salt, or to taste

^{1}/2 teaspoon freshly ground black pepper, or to taste

1 cup dry red wine (such as a Burgundy)

1^{1}/2 cups chicken broth

1 teaspoon dried thyme leaves

1 bay leaf

8 to 10 slices French bread, toasted on both sides

6 ounces imported Swiss cheese, grated (about 1^{1}/3 cups)

^{1}/4 cup freshly grated Parmesan cheese

2 tablespoons fresh flat-leaf parsley, chopped

In a 5-quart ovenproof casserole, melt the butter and sauté the onions until they become translucent, about 2–3 minutes. Add the mushrooms and garlic, and continue to sauté for 2 to 3 minutes. Remove the onions and mushrooms from the pan, and set them aside. Sprinkle the chicken pieces with 1 teaspoon salt and ^{1}/2 teaspoon pepper, and add them to the pan, browning the chicken on all sides for about 5 minutes. Return the vegetables to the pan, and deglaze the pan with the red wine, allowing the sauce to come to a boil. Add the broth, thyme, and bay leaf, taste the sauce, and correct the seasoning if necessary.

Partially cover the casserole, and simmer for 30 minutes, until the chicken is tender. (At this point remove the bay leaf and refrigerate the chicken for up to 2 days, or freeze it for up to 2 months.) If frozen, defrost the chicken overnight in the refrigerator and then reheat to serving temperature before covering with the croutons.

Preheat the broiler for 10 minutes. Place the toasted bread on top of the chicken, cutting it to fit in 1 layer. Sprinkle the bread evenly with the cheeses, and broil until the cheeses are melted. Remove from the oven, garnish with the parsley, and serve.

Serves 6 to 8

Lemon Herbed Chicken with
Grilled Vegetable Topping

A citrus marinade flavors the chicken and vegetables for this unusual pie. The vegetables cover the chicken to seal in the juices and produce a delicious low-fat entrée.

CHICKEN FILLING
8 skinless and boneless chicken breast halves

1/4 cup freshly squeezed lemon juice

2 teaspoons freshly grated lemon zest

2 tablespoons extra virgin olive oil

2 cloves garlic, minced

1 teaspoon dried oregano

1 teaspoon dried basil

1 teaspoon salt

1/2 teaspoon freshly ground black pepper

1 recipe Grilled Vegetable Topping (see below)

2 tablespoons olive oil

Place the chicken in a shallow dish. In a small bowl, combine the lemon juice, zest, olive oil, garlic, oregano, basil, salt, and pepper, stirring to combine. Pour the mixture over the chicken, turning the chicken in the marinade to coat it evenly. Cover with plastic wrap and refrigerate for 2 hours.

Make the crust.

To assemble, preheat the oven to 400° F. In a 12-inch sauté pan, heat the oil. Drain the chicken from the marinade and sauté it in the oil until it is browned on both sides, 3 minutes a side. Place the chicken in an ovenproof baking dish that will hold it in one layer. Arrange the grilled vegetables on top of the chicken. Bake in the preheated oven for 12 to 15 minutes until the chicken is tender and the juices are clear when the chicken is pierced with a sharp knife.

Grilled Vegetable Topping

2 small zucchini, cut lengthwise into $1/2$-inch slices

2 medium Japanese eggplants, or 1 medium purple eggplant, cut into $1/4$-inch-thick
rounds

1 purple onion, cut into $1/2$-inch rounds

1 red bell pepper, cored and sliced into 1-inch pieces

$1/4$ cup olive oil

$1/2$ teaspoon salt

$1/4$ teaspoon freshly ground pepper

Preheat the broiler or gas grill for 10 minutes. If you are doing the vegetables in the oven, arrange them in a foil-lined baking sheet. Brush them with the $1/4$ cup of oil and sprinkle them with the salt and pepper. Broil until they are softened, about 5 minutes. If you are cooking the vegetables on the grill, brush the vegetables with additional oil, salt, and pepper, before placing them on the grill. Grill until they are softened, 2–3 minutes on each side.

Serves 6 to 8

Lone Star Chicken Chili Topped with Refried Bean Crust

*C*hili *gets a new look made with chicken instead of beef and covered with a crust of refried beans enriched with sour cream and spices. Serve this for a football night gathering and your dinner may be the star of the game. We like to accompany this with Lone Star beer.*

CHILI

2 tablespoons vegetable oil

4 cups chicken cut into $1/2$-inch pieces (4 skinless and boneless half breasts)

2 cups chopped onions

4 cloves garlic, minced

1 tablespoon chili powder

2 teaspoons dried oregano

2 teaspoons ground cumin

1 cup beer

3 cups chicken broth

2 cups tomato sauce

$1/4$ cup masa harina

$1/4$ cup warm water

1 recipe Refried Bean Crust (see below)

2 cups grated Cheddar cheese

In a large stockpot, heat the oil, add the chicken, and sauté until the chicken is browned on all sides, about 6–8 minutes. Add the onions, garlic, chili powder, oregano, and cumin, stirring and cooking for 4 to 5 minutes, making sure that the onions do not brown. Slowly pour in the beer, chicken broth, and tomato sauce, stirring the bottom of the pot. Bring the mixture to a boil, and simmer, uncovered, for 45 minutes. Combine the masa with the water, and whisk until smooth. Gradually add the masa mixture to the chili, stirring until the mixture thickens slightly, simmering another 5 minutes. At this point the chili may be refrigerated for 3 days, or frozen for 2 months.

When you are ready to bake the chili, preheat the oven to 375° F. Place the chili in a 5-quart ovenproof casserole. Spread the beans over the chili, cover with the Cheddar cheese, and bake for 35 to 45 minutes, until the cheese is melted and the chili is bubbling.

Refried Bean Crust

3 (15-ounce) cans refried beans

1 teaspoon chili powder

6 shakes Tabasco or hot sauce

$1/2$ cup sour cream

Place the refried beans in a large mixing bowl or in the food processor. Add the other ingredients, and stir or process until the beans are smooth and the ingredients are combined. Refrigerate the crust until ready to bake the chili.

Serves 6 to 8

Ryan's Pie

*M*y son Ryan loves this pie. He's been known to eat most of it at the table, and then polish off the leftovers later in the evening. Made with chicken meat in a creamy thyme-flavored sauce, it's Mom's pot pie, but the crust is puff pastry. If you have leftover chicken from another meal, this goes together in no time. If you would like to make individual pies, pour 1 cup of filling into individual crocks or ramekins, and cut the puff pastry to fit the individual pies.

4 tablespoons butter

5 tablespoons flour, plus additional for rolling the pastry

2½ cups chicken broth

1 teaspoon chopped fresh thyme, or ½ teaspoon dried

½ teaspoon salt

¼ teaspoon freshly ground black pepper

½ cup heavy cream or milk

6 cups cooked chicken cut into ½-inch pieces

1 sheet puff pastry, defrosted

Preheat the oven 400° F. In a 4-quart saucepan, melt the butter and whisk in the 5 tablespoons of flour. Whisk about 2 minutes, until white bubbles begin to form on the top of the mixture. Gradually whisk in the broth, stirring until thick and smooth, about 4–6 minutes. Add the thyme, salt, pepper, and cream. Whisk until blended. Add the chicken. Pour the filling into a 13 by 9-inch oven-proof baking dish. (At this point, the filling may be refrigerated until ready to bake for up to 2 days. Bring back to room temperature before baking.) Sprinkle the puff pastry with 2 tablespoons of flour and roll it out to fit the baking dish. Drape the pastry over the filling and crimp the edges with the tines of a fork. Bake for 25 minutes, until the pastry is puffed and golden.

Serves 6 to 8

Tuscan Chicken Topped with Roasted Red Potato Crust

*M*y *grandmother's chicken gets a make-over with this crust of golden-brown, garlic-flavored red potatoes.*

8 boneless chicken thighs

3 teaspoons salt

$1^1/2$ teaspoons freshly ground black pepper

5 tablespoons olive oil

4 cloves garlic, mashed, plus 3 cloves slivered

$^1/3$ cup balsamic vinegar

$^1/2$ cup chicken broth

2 teaspoons dried rosemary

3 cups red potatoes sliced $^1/4$ inch thick

Sprinkle the chicken with 1 teaspoon of the salt and $^1/2$ teaspoon of the pepper. In a 3-quart Dutch oven, heat 2 tablespoons of the olive oil and sauté the chicken until it is browned on all sides, about 3 minutes on each side. Add the mashed garlic, and deglaze the pan with the balsamic vinegar. Shake the pan to loosen any browned bits that have formed on the bottom.

Add the chicken broth and rosemary, turning the chicken in the sauce. Cover the casserole and simmer for 10 minutes.

Preheat the oven to 400° F. Pour the remaining 3 tablespoons of olive oil, the garlic slivers, 2 teaspoons of salt and 1 teaspoon of pepper into a large bowl or Ziploc bag. Add the potatoes and toss to coat them with the mixture. Spread the potatoes in an even layer over the chicken in the casserole. Transfer to the oven and bake for 45 minutes, until the potatoes are golden brown. To serve, slice into the potatoes, and serve each person one piece of chicken on a bed of potatoes, spooning some of the pan juices over the chicken.

Serves 6 to 8

Moroccan Chicken Pie

B'*stilla is a Moroccan pot pie flavored with the spices of the Casbah and eaten with your hands! Now, how much more fun would dinner be if you let your family eat dinner without knives and forks? If you absolutely must have knives and forks, that's okay, but however you eat it, do try this fragrant and delicious pie covered with flaky phyllo. You can make it ahead of time, and it's a great conversation piece for a special dinner with friends.*

3 cups chicken broth

$1/8$ teaspoon saffron

2 cloves garlic, mashed

2 cinnamon sticks

$1/2$ teaspoon ground coriander

$1/4$ teaspoon ground turmeric

$1/2$ cup finely chopped onion

$1/2$ cup finely chopped carrot

$1/2$ cup finely minced flat-leaf parsley

8 eggs, lightly beaten

3 tablespoons butter

$1^{1}/2$ cups blanched almonds

$1/3$ cup confectioners' sugar, plus additional for sprinkling

1 teaspoon ground cinnamon, plus additional for sprinkling

1 pound frozen phyllo sheets, thawed

$3/4$ cup melted butter

$1/2$ cup dry bread crumbs

4 cups cooked chicken diced into $1/2$-inch pieces

In a 4-quart saucepan, heat the chicken broth. Add the saffron, garlic, cinnamon sticks, coriander, turmeric, onion, and carrot. Bring the broth to a boil and simmer, uncovered, for 20 minutes. Remove the cinnamon sticks from the broth and lower the heat to medium. Stir in the parsley and eggs, stirring the eggs until they appear like scrambled eggs, but not dry. Remove the eggs and vegetables with a slotted spoon and place them in a colander set over a bowl. (Refrigerate until ready to proceed.)

In a heavy sauté pan, melt the butter. Add the almonds and brown them in the butter, being careful not to burn them. Remove from the heat, and cool. Place the almonds in a food processor fitted with a metal blade, add the $1/3$ cup confectioners' sugar and the 1 teaspoon ground cinnamon, and pulse on and off until the almonds are ground. Set aside until ready to proceed.

Preheat the oven to 400° F. Unwrap the phyllo and cover it with a clean kitchen towel. Brush a 13 by 9-inch ovenproof baking dish with melted butter. Brush a sheet of phyllo with melted butter, sprinkle it with some of the bread crumbs, and place it in the baking dish. Repeat with 5 more sheets of phyllo, brushing each one with butter and sprinkling it with crumbs. (You will have 6 sheets total.) Spread half the egg and vegetable mixture over the phyllo, and sprinkle the filling with half the ground almonds. Cover with 2 more sheets of phyllo brushed with butter and sprinkled with bread crumbs. Cover with all the chicken, then top with 2 more sheets of phyllo brushed with butter and sprinkled with bread crumbs. Top with the remaining egg and vegetable mixture and the remaining ground almonds. Cover the pie with 4 more sheets of phyllo, each buttered and sprinkled with bread crumbs. (At this point the pie may be refrigerated for up to 24 hours before baking.)

Bake for 30 to 40 minutes, until the phyllo is golden brown. Remove the pie from the oven and let it rest for 5 minutes. Sprinkle with powdered sugar and ground cinnamon and serve.

Serves 8

Not Your Mother's Chicken Divan

*T*his wonderful casserole, taken from those pot luck suppers of the '50s that layered chicken, broccoli, and cream soup, becomes a pie for the Millennium when the chicken and broccoli are cooked in a curry-flavored sauce and topped with a thick Cheddar crumb crust. Easy, delicious, and a great do-ahead, you could even serve this to the boss.

CHICKEN FILLING
3 tablespoons butter
1 tablespoon vegetable oil
8 skinless and boneless chicken breast halves
1 teaspoon salt
$1/2$ teaspoon freshly ground black pepper
3 cups broccoli florets, steamed al dente
3 tablespoons flour
$1^1/2$ teaspoons curry powder
2 cups chicken broth
$1/2$ cup milk

1 recipe Cheddar Crumb Crust (see below)

In a sauté pan, heat 1 tablespoon of the butter with the vegetable oil. Sprinkle the chicken with the salt and pepper and sauté until it is golden on both sides but not cooked through, 3 minutes on each side. Arrange the chicken in the bottom of an ovenproof baking dish and top it with the broccoli. Melt the remaining 2 tablespoons of butter in the same pan and whisk in the flour and curry powder until the mixture begins to bubble, about 3 to 4 minutes. Gradually add the chicken broth, and whisk until smooth. Add the milk, and bring the sauce to a boil. Pour the sauce over the chicken and broccoli. (Refrigerate until ready to bake.) Preheat the 375° F. Make the crust. Spread the crust over the chicken and broccoli and bake for 20 to 25 minutes, until the crust is golden and the sauce is bubbling.

Cheddar Crumb Crust

4 tablespoons butter
3½ cups fresh French bread crumbs
2 cups freshly grated Cheddar cheese

In a sauté pan, melt the butter. Add the bread crumbs, and stir until the crumbs are crisp, about 4–5 minutes. Remove the crumbs to a mixing bowl and add the Cheddar cheese, tossing to distribute the ingredients evenly. Spread the crust over the chicken and broccoli and bake for 20 to 25 minutes, until the crust is golden and the sauce is bubbling.

Serves 6 to 8

Old-Fashioned Chicken Pot Pie with Chive Mashed Potato Crust

*T*his pot pie is like Mom's, except that I've topped it with chive mashed potatoes. Try using Yukon Gold potatoes for a beautifully golden crust. The filling and the mashed potato crust can be made up ahead of time, and then baked.

CHICKEN FILLING

4 tablespoons butter

$1/4$ cup finely chopped onion

5 tablespoons flour

3 cups chicken broth

1 cup carrots cut into $1/2$-inch dice

1 teaspoon salt

$1/2$ teaspoon freshly ground black pepper

1 teaspoon chopped fresh sage, or $1/2$ teaspoon dried

1 cup milk

1 cup fresh, or frozen, defrosted corn kernels

1 cup fresh or frozen and defrosted petite peas

2 cups cooked chicken

1 recipe Chive Mashed Potatoes (see below)

In a 4-quart saucepan, melt the butter and sauté the onion for 2 minutes, until it begins to soften. Add the flour, and whisk until it bubbles. Gradually whisk in the broth, stirring until the sauce is thick and smooth, about 3–5 minutes. Add the carrots, salt, pepper, and sage, stirring until the sauce begins to simmer. Simmer for 5 minutes. Add the milk, corn, peas, and chicken, simmering for another 3 minutes. Pour the filling into a 3-quart casserole. Refrigerate until ready to bake.

Make the crust.

Preheat the oven to 375° F. Bake the pot pie for 30 to 40 minutes, until the potatoes are golden brown.

Chive Mashed Potatoes

2½ pounds russet potatoes, peeled and cut in 1-inch cubes

5 tablespoons butter

1 teaspoon salt

¼ teaspoon freshly ground black pepper

2 tablespoons chopped fresh chives

¼ cup heavy cream

Place the potatoes in a 4-quart saucepan with water to cover. Boil the potatoes for 15 to 20 minutes, until they are tender when pierced with a knife. Drain the potatoes and return them to the hot pan. Shake the pan over medium heat to dry the potatoes. Add 4 tablespoons of the butter, the salt, pepper, and chives, mashing the potatoes to the desired degree of smoothness. Blend in the cream, and stir to combine. Spread the potatoes over the chicken filling and dot with the remaining 1 tablespoon of butter.

Serves 6 to 8

Oriental Chicken and Vegetables Topped with Noodle Pancake

You'll know this isn't your mother's pot pie when you stir-fry the ingredients, and then top it with the noodle pancake. The chicken and veggies can be cut up and made ready ahead of time, while the noodle pancake can be made with any leftover noodles, and cooked just before serving. Bring the wok to the table, cut each portion, laying the pancake on the plate first, covering it with the chicken and vegetables. If you would like to substitute beef, or make it vegetarian, that can be done, too.

NOODLE PANCAKE

1 tablespoon vegetable oil

1 tablespoons sesame oil

$1/2$ pound angel hair pasta, cooked al dente and drained

CHICKEN AND VEGETABLE STIR-FRY

$1/2$ cup chicken broth

$1/4$ cup soy sauce

2 teaspoons cornstarch

1 tablespoon vegetable oil

1 tablespoon sesame oil

2 cloves garlic, mashed

1 tablespoon chopped fresh ginger

1 whole chicken breast cut into $1/2$-inch dice (about 2 cups)

1 large onion, thinly sliced

1 cup sliced shiitake mushrooms

1 carrot, cut on the diagonal into $1/2$-inch slices (about 1 cup)

1 cup broccoli florets

1 cup fresh spinach leaves

To make the pancake, in a 10- or 12-inch non-stick skillet, heat the oils over high heat. When the oil is hot, add the pasta in one layer. The oil will spatter a bit, so be careful. When the bottom of the pancake has begun to brown, turn the pancake over, and cook until it is crisp. Remove from the skillet, drain on paper towels, and keep warm in a low oven.

In a small bowl, combine the broth, soy sauce and cornstarch and set aside. In a wok over high heat, heat the vegetable and sesame oils. Add the garlic and ginger, stirring for 30 seconds. Add the chicken, and cook until it turns white on all sides, about 4 minutes, tossing frequently. Remove the chicken from the pan and add the onion and mushrooms, stir-frying for 2 minutes. Add the carrot, broccoli, and the reserved chicken to the pan and stir-fry for another 2 minutes. Add the spinach, and then pour in the reserved broth mixture, stirring to coat all the ingredients. When the sauce is thickened, in 2–3 minutes, remove the wok from the heat.

Top the stir-fry with the noodle pancake. Serve immediately.

Serves 6

Turkey Cassoulet with Puree of White Beans, Garlic, Parmesan, and Parsley Crust

Does your family turn up their noses at the mention of beans? They will never suspect that the fabulous crust covering this rich turkey and sausage stew is made from a puree of white beans. The stew and crust can be prepared ahead of time and refrigerated for up to 2 days. The cassoulet can be frozen for up to 1 month. This is a great warm-up on a cold winter night, or a wonderful welcome-home after a day of skiing.

TURKEY FILLING

$^1/_2$ cup all-purpose flour

2 teaspoons salt, plus additional to taste

$^1/_2$ teaspoon freshly ground black pepper, plus additional to taste

2 pounds turkey tenderloin, cut into $1^1/_2$-inch chunks

2 tablespoons olive oil

1 cup boneless pork loin cut into 1-inch chunks (about $^1/_2$ pound)

1 pound smoked sausage, cut into 1-inch rounds

6 cloves garlic, minced

2 large onions, sliced $^1/_2$-inch-thick

$^1/_2$ cup chopped tomatoes

1 teaspoon dried thyme

1 bay leaf

1 cup dry red wine

2 cups chicken broth

1 recipe White Bean Crust (see below)

Combine the flour, 2 teaspoons of salt, and $^1/_2$ teaspoon of pepper in a Ziploc bag. Add the turkey, seal the bag, and shake until the turkey is coated. In a 5-quart Dutch oven or ovenproof casserole, heat the oil, add the turkey, and cook until a golden crust forms on all sides, about 6–8 minutes. Remove the turkey from the casserole, add the pork and sausage, and brown the meats on all sides. Return the turkey to the casserole along with the garlic and onions. Sauté until the onions become translucent, about 4–6 minutes. Add the tomatoes, thyme, bay leaf, and red wine, bringing the mixture to a boil. Stir up the browned bits on the bottom of the pan and add the broth. Reduce the heat and simmer the stew, covered, for 1 hour, until the meats are tender. When the stew is finished, skim off any fat from the top of the broth and reseason the cassoulet with salt and pepper to taste.

Preheat the oven to 400° F. Prepare the crust.

Bake the cassoulet for 20 minutes, until the top is golden. Serve immediately.

White Bean Crust

2 tablespoons butter

1 clove garlic, mashed

$1/2$ cup dry bread crumbs

2 tablespoons chopped fresh flat-leaf parsley

$1/4$ cup freshly grated Parmesan cheese

1 (15-ounce) can small white beans, drained and rinsed

$1/4$ cup chicken broth

Salt and freshly ground black pepper to taste

In a small sauté pan, melt the butter. Add the garlic and sauté until it's soft, about 2–3 minutes. Add the bread crumbs, parsley, and Parmesan cheese, stirring to coat all ingredients with the butter. Set aside.

Place the beans in a large mixing bowl, or in the food processor. Mash the beans, adding the chicken broth to help make a smooth paste. Season the beans with salt and pepper. Using a large spatula, flatten some of the bean mixture, and slide the beans onto the cassoulet, repeating until the "crust" covers the cassoulet. Sprinkle the top with the bread crumb mixture.

Serves 8

Turkey Meat Loaf Surprise

*W*hen I was in college, any time the main course contained the word "surprise," we knew it wasn't going to be a pleasant one. This meat loaf's surprise is the addition of applesauce to make it moist, as well as the bacon and sour cream mashed potato crust. This is a tasty, quick main course.

MEAT LOAF FILLING

2 pounds ground turkey

1 1/2 teaspoons salt

1/2 teaspoon freshly ground black pepper

1/2 cup applesauce

1/2 cup finely chopped onion

1/2 cup ketchup

2 teaspoons Worcestershire sauce

2 teaspoons chopped fresh thyme, or 1 teaspoon dried

1 teaspoon chopped fresh sage leaves, or 1/2 teaspoon dried

1/2 cup fresh bread crumbs

1 recipe Bacon Sour Cream Mashed Potatoes (see below)

2 tablespoons butter

Grease a 10-inch round ovenproof baking dish. Place all the filling ingredients in a mixing bowl and stir until combined. Spread the turkey mixture into the prepared baking dish. Refrigerate until ready to bake.

Make the mashed potatoes.

When ready to proceed, preheat the oven to 375° F. Spread the potatoes over the meat loaf, dot the top with the butter, and place in the preheated oven. Bake for 45 minutes to 1 hour, until the potatoes are golden brown. Cut into wedges and serve.

Bacon Sour Cream Mashed Potatoes

4 medium russet potatoes, peeled and cut into 1-inch cubes

2 teaspoons salt

$^{1}/_{2}$ pound bacon, cut into $^{1}/_{2}$-inch strips, cooked until crisp

4 tablespoons milk

$^{1}/_{2}$ cup sour cream

1 teaspoon freshly ground black pepper

Place the potatoes in a 4-quart saucepan with water to cover. Add 1 teaspoon of the salt and bring the water to a boil. Boil gently for 15 to 20 minutes, until the potatoes are tender when pierced with a sharp knife. Drain the potatoes in a colander and return them to the pan. Shake the pan over the heat to dry the potatoes. Add the remaining teaspoon of salt, the bacon, milk, sour cream, and pepper. Mash the potatoes, and taste to correct the seasoning. Cool the potatoes in the refrigerator until ready to bake.

Serves 6 to 8

Turkey Orlof with Creamy Onion Rice Topping

*T*his elegant pie is a simple adaptation of a complicated veal dish. This version uses turkey cutlets and covers them with a rich mushroom, onion, and rice crust. If you have leftover turkey from a holiday dinner, substitute cooked turkey meat for the cutlets, top with the crust, and bake as directed. The entire dish can be made 2 days ahead of time, refrigerated, then baked right before serving.

$^3/_4$ cup all-purpose flour

$1^1/_2$ teaspoons salt

1 teaspoon freshly ground black pepper

10 ($^1/_2$-inch-thick) slices turkey breast

1 tablespoon olive oil

6 tablespoons butter

1 large onion, finely chopped

1 pound button mushrooms, washed and sliced $^1/_2$ inch thick

1 teaspoon chopped fresh tarragon

$2^1/_2$ cups chicken broth

$^1/_2$ cup milk

2 tablespoons sherry

2 cups cooked long-grain rice

$1^1/_2$ cups freshly grated imported Swiss cheese

In a flat dish, combine $^1/_2$ cup of flour, 1 teaspoon of salt, and $^1/_2$ teaspoon of pepper. Dip the turkey slices into the flour mixture, setting them aside when coated. Grease a 13 by 9-inch ovenproof casserole.

In a 12-inch sauté pan, melt the olive oil with 2 tablespoons of the butter. Add the turkey, a few slices at a time to avoid crowding. When the turkey is browned on both sides, remove it to the casserole. Continue to brown the turkey until all the slices are done.

Melt the remaining butter in the same sauté pan, add the onion, until it becomes translucent, 3–4 minutes. Add the mushrooms, seasoning with the remaining salt and pepper and the tarragon. Cook until the mushrooms begin to give off some of their moisture, 3–5 minutes. Sprinkle the mushrooms with the remaining 4 tablespoons of flour, stirring until the flour begins to bubble on the bottom of the pan. Gradually add the chicken broth, whisking the sauce until it is smooth. When the sauce begins to boil, turn down the heat to medium, and add the milk and sherry. (If you are not finishing the dish right away, refrigerate the turkey and the sauce separately.)

When ready to serve, preheat the oven to 375° F. Stir the rice into the sauce mixture and pour it over the turkey. Sprinkle the Swiss cheese over the top, and bake for 20 to 25 minutes, until the sauce is bubbling and the cheese is melted and golden brown. Serve immediately.

Serves 6 to 8

...th Cranberry Thyme Crust

...an awesome combination. This recipe uses dried cranberries
...ust to set off the rich turkey filling.

TURKEY FILLING
2 tablespoons butter
$1/2$ cup finely chopped onion
$1/2$ cup finely chopped celery
$1/2$ cup finely chopped carrot
2 tablespoons all-purpose flour
2 cups chicken or turkey broth
$1/2$ cup milk
4 cups cut-up cooked turkey or chicken meat
1 teaspoon chopped fresh thyme, or $1/2$ teaspoon dried
1 teaspoon salt
$1/2$ teaspoon freshly ground black pepper

1 recipe Cranberry Thyme Crust (see below)

In a 3-quart saucepan, melt the butter, add the onion, celery, and carrot, and sauté for 2 minutes. Sprinkle the flour over the vegetables and cook until white bubbles begin to form, about 2–3 minutes. Gradually whisk in the broth and milk, stirring until the sauce is smooth and thick, about 4–6 minutes. Add the turkey, thyme, salt, and pepper, and taste the sauce for seasoning. Transfer the filling to a 10-inch round ovenproof baking dish.

Preheat the oven to 400° F. Make the crust.

Pour the mixture over the turkey pie and bake for 30 minutes, until the crust is golden.

Cranberry Thyme Crust

1^1/$_2$ cups Bisquick

^{3}/$_4$ cup milk

1 egg

^{1}/$_2$ cup dried cranberries

1 teaspoon dried thyme

Place the Bisquick in a mixing bowl. Add the remaining ingredients and stir until combined.

Serves 6 to 8

Turkey Pot Pie with Onion Sage Dressing

*T*urkey *and dressing are my family's favorite part of Thanksgiving dinner, so you can imagine their delight when I came up with this pie. Now we can have our favorites all year round. This is a great way to use leftover French bread and cooked turkey or chicken.*

TURKEY FILLING

3 tablespoons butter

1 cup sliced mushrooms

3 tablespoons all-purpose flour

2$^{1}/_{2}$ cups chicken or turkey broth

2 cups cut-up cooked turkey or chicken

1 cup fresh peas, or frozen and defrosted petite peas

$^{1}/_{2}$ cup finely diced carrot

1 teaspoon chopped fresh sage, or $^{1}/_{2}$ teaspoon dried

Salt and freshly ground black pepper, to taste

1 recipe Onion Sage Dressing (see below)

2 tablespoons melted butter

In a 2-quart saucepan, melt the butter. Add the mushrooms and sauté until they give off some of their liquid, about 4–6 minutes. Sprinkle the mushrooms with the flour and stir until the flour is cooked and small bubbles form on the bottom of the pan, about 2–3 minutes. Gradually whisk in the broth, stirring until smooth. When the broth begins to boil, reduce the heat and stir in the turkey, peas, carrot, and sage. Taste the sauce and adjust the seasoning with salt and pepper. (At this point, the filling may be refrigerated for up to 2 days, or frozen for up to 1 month.)

Preheat the oven to 375° F. Make the dressing.

Place the turkey mixture in a 3-quart or 13 by 9-inch casserole dish, cover it with the dressing, and sprinkle the top with the melted butter. Bake for 30 to 45 minutes, until the dressing is golden brown and the turkey filling is bubbly.

Onion Sage Dressing

4 tablespoons butter
$^1/_2$ cup chopped onion
$^1/_2$ cup chopped celery
1 teaspoon fresh sage leaves, or $^1/_2$ teaspoon dried
$^1/_2$ teaspoon fresh thyme leaves, or $^1/_4$ teaspoon dried
4 cups dry French bread crumbs
$^1/_2$ cup chicken or turkey broth

In a sauté pan, melt the butter and add the onion, celery, sage, and thyme. Sauté for about 3 minutes, until the vegetables are soft. Place the bread crumbs in a mixing bowl. Add the onion-celery mixture and toss well. Add some of the chicken broth, a few tablespoons at a time, to moisten the bread crumbs. If you like your dressing moist, add all of the broth; if you like it drier, add just enough to suit your taste.

Serves 6 to 8

Turkey Squash Pie with White Cheddar and Bacon Crust

*Y*ellow squash and zucchini combine to make a colorful filling for this delicious pie with an unusual white Cheddar and bacon corn bread crust. A great way to use leftover turkey or chicken. Add any leftover vegetables to the filling as well.

TURKEY SQUASH FILLING
2 tablespoons butter

3 small zucchini, cut into $1/2$-inch-thick rounds

3 small yellow squash, cut into $1/2$-inch-thick chunks

$1/2$ cup finely chopped carrot

2 tablespoons all-purpose flour

2 cups chicken broth

4 cups cooked turkey or chicken meat cut into bite-sized pieces

$1/2$ teaspoon salt

$1/4$ teaspoon freshly ground black pepper

1 teaspoon chopped fresh sage, or $1/2$ teaspoon dried

1 recipe White Cheddar and Bacon Crust (see below)

In a 4-quart saucepan, melt the butter and add the zucchini, squash, and carrot. Sauté the vegetables for 2 minutes, then sprinkle with the flour. Stir the mixture until the flour begins to bubble. Whisk in the broth, and stir until the sauce is thick and smooth, about 4–6 minutes. Stir in the turkey or chicken, the salt, pepper, and sage. Transfer the mixture to a 3-quart ovenproof baking dish.

Preheat the oven to 350° F. Make the crust.

Bake the pie in the preheated oven for 30 minutes, until the pie is browned and bubbling.

White Cheddar and Bacon Crust

¹/₄ cup butter

¹/₂ cup chopped green onion

2 cups crumbled corn bread

8 slices bacon, cooked, drained, and crumbled

1 cup freshly grated white Cheddar cheese

¹/₄ cup chicken broth, or as needed

In a sauté pan, heat the butter and add the green onion. Sauté for 2 minutes, until the onion begins to soften. Place the corn bread in a large mixing bowl. Transfer the onion-butter mixture to the bowl along with the bacon and Cheddar cheese. Drizzle some of the broth over the corn bread to moisten it. When the mixture is crumbly, sprinkle it over the turkey in the baking dish.

Serves 6 to 8

Turkey Vegetable Dill Pie with Chive Biscuit Crust

*S*ometimes leftover turkey seems like it is multiplying every time you open the refrigerator door. After all, how many turkey sandwiches can one person eat? Fragrant with dill in a creamy, rich vegetable sauce, and covered with light-as-a-feather chive biscuits, this delectable pie will take the boredom out of that leftover turkey.

TURKEY VEGETABLE FILLING

4 tablespoons butter

1 cup finely chopped carrots

1/2 cup finely chopped celery

3 tablespoons flour

2 1/2 cups chicken broth

1 teaspoon salt, plus additional to taste

1/2 teaspoon freshly ground black pepper, plus additional to taste

1/2 cup heavy cream

4 cups cooked turkey meat cut into 1-inch chunks

1 cup fresh, or frozen and defrosted petite green peas

1/2 cup fresh, or frozen and defrosted corn kernels

1 tablespoon fresh dillweed, or 1 1/2 teaspoons dried

1 recipe Chive Biscuit Crust (see below)

Cranberry sauce, for serving

In a 4-quart saucepan, melt the butter. Add the carrots and celery, and sauté for 3 to 4 minutes. Sprinkle the flour over the vegetables and stir until the flour begins to form bubbles on the bottom of the pan. Whisk in the chicken broth, stirring until the sauce is smooth and begins to boil. Season it with 1 teaspoon of salt and 1/2 teaspoon of pepper, reduce the heat to a simmer, and add the cream, turkey, vegetables, and dill. Cook the mixture for 5 minutes, until the sauce is thickened. Taste it and correct the seasoning with additional salt and pepper if necessary.

Place the filling in a 4-quart casserole or a 13 by 9-inch ovenproof baking dish. (The filling may be refrigerated for 2 days before baking. If you would like to freeze this, do not add the cream, and freeze for 1 month.)

Preheat the oven to 375° F. Make the crust.

Bake the pie for 20 to 25 minutes, until the biscuits are browned and the pie is bubbling. Serve with cranberry sauce.

Chive Biscuit Crust
2 cups all-purpose flour
1 tablespoon baking powder
2 tablespoons fresh snipped chives
1/2 teaspoon salt
1/3 cup vegetable shortening
3/4 cup milk

In a large mixing bowl, combine the flour, baking powder, chives, and salt. Cut in the shortening until the mixture resembles small peas. Stirring with a fork, add the milk, a few tablespoons at a time, and stop when the mixture begins to come together. Turn the dough out onto a floured board, and knead it 4 to 5 times. Pat the dough into a circle, and roll it out 1/2 inch thick. Cut it into biscuits and top the pie with the biscuits. Reroll and cut any scraps.

Serves 6 to 8

Monte Cristo Pie

*O*ne *of my daughter Carrie's favorite restaurant foods is a classic Monte Cristo sand-*
wich. I created this pie so we could enjoy her favorite at home.

1 (1-pound) loaf good sandwich-type bread, crusts removed
³/₄ pound Black Forest ham, thinly sliced
³/₄ pound thinly sliced turkey, or 3 cups cooked cubed turkey
³/₄ pound sliced Swiss cheese, plus ¹/₂ cup grated
10 eggs
2¹/₄ cups milk
1 cup heavy cream
1 teaspoon salt
¹/₄ teaspoon freshly ground black pepper
3 tablespoons melted butter

Grease a 13 by 9-inch ovenproof casserole dish. Place one third of the bread slices in the casserole, to make a single layer. Top the bread with half the ham, turkey, and sliced cheese. Repeat with another layer of bread, ham, turkey, and cheese. Use the remaining third of the bread for the top crust.

In a large mixing bowl, whisk together the eggs, milk, cream, salt, and pepper. Pour the mixture over the layers of bread in the casserole, tilting the casserole to make sure the liquid is evenly distributed. Brush the top with melted butter and cover the dish with plastic wrap. Refrigerate the casserole for 12 hours, or up to 24 hours before baking.

Preheat the oven to 350° F. Remove the plastic wrap from the casserole, sprinkle the top with the grated Swiss cheese, and bake the pie for 45 to 55 minutes, until it's puffed and golden. Remove from the oven, allow to stand for 5 minutes, and cut into squares to serve.

Serves 6 to 8

Meat
Pot Pies

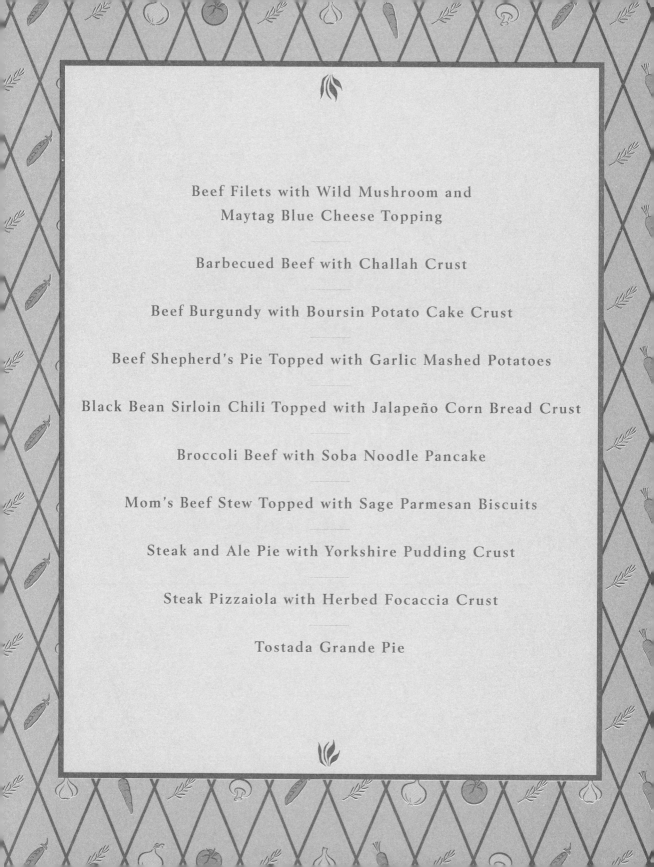

Beef Filets with Wild Mushroom and
Maytag Blue Cheese Topping

Barbecued Beef with Challah Crust

Beef Burgundy with Boursin Potato Cake Crust

Beef Shepherd's Pie Topped with Garlic Mashed Potatoes

Black Bean Sirloin Chili Topped with Jalapeño Corn Bread Crust

Broccoli Beef with Soba Noodle Pancake

Mom's Beef Stew Topped with Sage Parmesan Biscuits

Steak and Ale Pie with Yorkshire Pudding Crust

Steak Pizzaiola with Herbed Focaccia Crust

Tostada Grande Pie

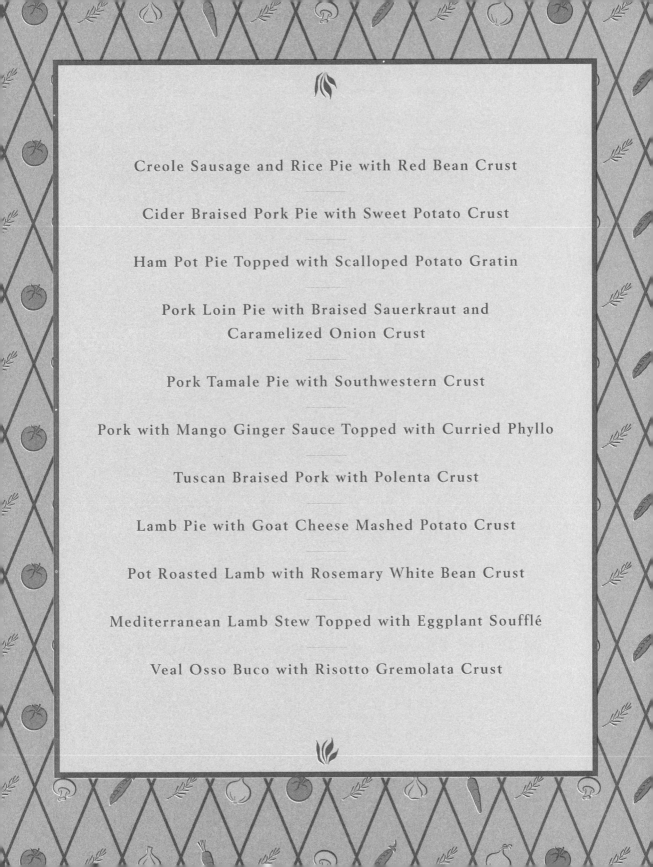

Creole Sausage and Rice Pie with Red Bean Crust

Cider Braised Pork Pie with Sweet Potato Crust

Ham Pot Pie Topped with Scalloped Potato Gratin

Pork Loin Pie with Braised Sauerkraut and
Caramelized Onion Crust

Pork Tamale Pie with Southwestern Crust

Pork with Mango Ginger Sauce Topped with Curried Phyllo

Tuscan Braised Pork with Polenta Crust

Lamb Pie with Goat Cheese Mashed Potato Crust

Pot Roasted Lamb with Rosemary White Bean Crust

Mediterranean Lamb Stew Topped with Eggplant Soufflé

Veal Osso Buco with Risotto Gremolata Crust

REMEMBER how delicious your mom's beef stew tasted on a cold and rainy night? Chockful of hearty beef and vegetables, it was a sign that all was right with the world. Served with potatoes or biscuits, this meal would make you and your tummy smile. We're going to do Mom's stew one better in this chapter by using beef, pork, or lamb to create hearty pies topped with everything from garlic mashed potatoes to eggplant soufflé.

Beef cuts that do well in pies are round, sirloin, and some stewing cuts. Unless otherwise stated, stewing cuts will take longer to cook than round or sirloin. To get a perfect pie like Mom used to make, take care to brown the meat evenly before adding the liquids for braising. This helps to ensure a deeper flavor in both meat and sauce. Season the meat before browning, and again during the cooking process, to ensure that the flavors are balanced. Since most pie fillings benefit from being made ahead, feel free to make these one or two days earlier than you need them, and refrigerate them until you are ready to serve.

Pork, the other white meat, is leaner and more tender than it used to be when used in pies. Even browning, as well as flavorful liquids, help to make rich gravies for these pies. I like to use pork tenderloin, and also boneless chops. If your grocer is having a sale on pork, it's a great idea to stock up, remove the bones, and freeze the meat in one- or two-pound packages.

I use chicken broth to flavor pork sauces, and sometimes add a bit of beef stock to make a heartier gravy. Pork combines well with fruits, so fruit nectars and juices can be used to flavor the sauces as well.

Lamb is a flavor some of us remember all too painfully from childhood, when Grandma would roast a leg of mutton, and force-feed us Sunday dinner. Today's lamb, leaner and more succulent, will liven up any dinner when paired with crusts made from white beans and rosemary or potato cakes. Buy boneless shoulder pieces, or a whole leg that has been boned, and cut the meat into one-inch chunks. Chicken and beef broth used in equal amounts, enhance lamb sauces very well. I find that using beef broth by itself overpowers the flavor of the lamb. Lamb is particularly delicious when cooked with red wine.

Meat pies that have rice, pasta, bread, or biscuit crusts need plenty of liquid, as the crust will absorb a lot during the final cooking. If the sauce looks thin, remember that it will thicken once the crust is baked. Since meat fillings require long, slow cooking, any fresh vegetables should be added toward the end of the cooking time so that they don't disintegrate.

Beef Filets with Wild Mushroom and Maytag Blue Cheese Topping

*T*his is inspired by a signature dish at Emeril's restaurant in New Orleans. The entire dish can be prepared the day before serving, refrigerated, and reheated.

1 tablespoon olive oil

6 filets mignons

2 teaspoons salt

1 teaspoon freshly ground black pepper

2 tablespoons butter

$1/2$ pound shiitake mushrooms, sliced $1/2$ inch thick

$1/2$ pound cremini mushrooms, sliced $1/2$ inch thick

1 tablespoon sherry

4 ounces crumbled Maytag blue cheese

2 egg yolks

1 tablespoon Worcestershire sauce

$1/2$ cup heavy cream

In a 10-inch sauté pan, heat the olive oil. Season the filets with half the salt and pepper, then add them to the hot skillet, searing them on both sides. Transfer the filets to a 13 by 9-inch baking dish. Meanwhile, melt the butter in the same skillet, add the mushrooms and the remaining salt and pepper. Sauté the mushrooms until they give off some of their moisture, about 5 minutes, then add the sherry to deglaze the pan. Spread the mushrooms over the filets, and refrigerate until ready to bake.

In a bowl, beat the blue cheese together with the egg yolks, Worcestershire, and heavy cream until smooth. Refrigerate the topping until ready to bake.

Preheat the oven to 400° F. Spread the blue cheese over the filets and mushrooms. Bake in the preheated oven for 8 to 10 minutes for medium rare. Remove the filets from the oven and serve at once.

Serves 6

Barbecued Beef with Challah Crust

*B*arbecued beef sandwiches are my son Ryan's favorite tail-gate food, and we usually serve them on challah rolls. The smoky sauce soaks into the eggy bread, and it's heaven. This pie takes a little time to make because the beef must roast before it is sliced into the barbecue sauce, covered with the egg bread dough, and baked. If you are planning to do this on a weekend, roast the beef a day ahead. You can make the barbecue sauce up to one month ahead and freeze it.

BEEF

1 teaspoon salt

1 clove garlic, mashed

$1/2$ teaspoon freshly ground black pepper

$2^1/2$ pounds beef brisket or tri-tip roast (sirloin tip roast)

BARBECUE SAUCE

2 tablespoons butter

1 cup chopped onion

2 cloves garlic, minced

3 (8-ounce) cans tomato sauce

$1/3$ cup brown sugar

2 teaspoons Worcestershire sauce

6 shakes Tabasco sauce

$1/2$ cup water, as needed

1 teaspoon salt

1 recipe Challah Crust (see below)

Preheat the oven to 325° F. Make a paste of the salt, garlic, and pepper, and spread it over the beef. Roast the meat in the preheated oven for 45 minutes. Let the meat rest for 15 minutes, then slice it on the diagonal $1/4$ inch thick.

In a 3-quart saucepan, heat the butter and sauté the onion and garlic for 2 to 3 minutes. Add the tomato sauce, brown sugar, Worcestershire, Tabasco, and any accumulated meat juices from the roasting pan. Cook the sauce for 10 minutes. Add some water if the sauce seems too thick. Season with the salt and cook for another 10 minutes. Layer the sauce and meat in an ovenproof baking dish.

Make the crust. Preheat the oven to 375° F.

Bake the pot pie in the preheated oven for 25 minutes, until the crust is golden.

Challah Crust

With apologies to those who take all day to make challah, this recipe is easy and only requires one rising. Saffron gives the bread a deeper golden color, but you can certainly omit it. Enjoy!

1 package rapid-rise yeast
4½ cups all-purpose flour (plus additional for kneading)
1 tablespoon sugar
1 teaspoon salt
½ cup warm water (105° F)
Pinch of saffron (optional)
3 tablespoons melted butter
3 egg yolks

In a mixing bowl, combine the yeast, flour, sugar, and salt. Dissolve the saffron (if you are using it) in the water. Add the water to the mixing bowl along with the butter and egg yolks. Stir the mixture until it forms a dough. Turn the dough out onto a floured board and knead it for 5 minutes. Place the dough in an oiled bowl, and let the dough rise in a warm place for 45 minutes. Preheat the oven to 375 degrees. Shape the dough into a crust or individual rolls to fit your baking dish. Place it on top of the beef and sauce.

Serves 8

Beef Burgundy with Boursin Potato Cake Crust

*T*ender *chunks of beef simmer in a hearty Burgundy wine sauce with mushrooms and onions. The pie is topped with mashed potato cakes, which absorb the juices from the stew and produce another pie fit for the boss.*

BEEF BURGUNDY FILLING

3 pounds lean beef sirloin, cut into $1\frac{1}{2}$- to 2-inch chunks

1 teaspoon salt

$\frac{1}{2}$ teaspoon freshly ground black pepper

3 cloves garlic, mashed

$1\frac{1}{2}$ tablespoons olive oil

2 cups Burgundy wine

2 cups beef broth

2 teaspoons dried thyme

1 bay leaf

2 tablespoons butter

6 medium onions, quartered

1 pound fresh button mushrooms, halved

3 tablespoons flour

$\frac{1}{4}$ cup warm water

1 recipe Boursin Potato Cakes (see below)

Preheat the oven to 325° F. Sprinkle the beef with the salt, pepper, and garlic. In a 5-quart Dutch oven, heat the oil and add the beef a few pieces at a time, browning it on all sides. Set the pieces aside as they are done. When all the beef is browned, return it to the pan, add the wine, and bring it to a boil. Add the broth, thyme, and bay leaf. Cover the pan, and bake the stew in the preheated oven for 30 minutes.

While the stew is cooking, melt the butter in a sauté pan, add the onions, and cook until they are golden and caramelized, about 10–15 minutes. Remove the onions to a plate, and add the mushrooms to the sauté pan, tossing them in the butter remaining in the pan. At the end of 30 minutes, add the onions and mushrooms to the stew. Remove the bay leaf at this time. Whisk together the flour and warm water and stir it into the stew. Cook for an additional 15 minutes.

Make the potato cakes. When ready to serve the pie, float the cakes onto the stew and bake for another 15 minutes. Serve immediately.

Boursin Potato Cakes

This is a great way to use leftover mashed potatoes. If you have instant mashed potatoes, they will work well in this recipe.

4 cups mashed potatoes (4 to 5 large baking potatoes, boiled and mashed)
1 (3-ounce) package Boursin cheese (or other garlic herb cheese)
2 egg yolks
2 to 4 tablespoons butter

Place the potatoes into a mixing bowl, and beat in the cheese and egg yolks. Form the mixture into cakes 3 inches in diameter and 1 inch thick. Melt half the butter in a sauté pan, and add the cakes, a few at a time, sautéing them until both sides are browned, about 3–4 minutes on each side. Repeat, adding more butter to the pan as needed, until all the potato is used. (Refrigerate until ready to proceed.)

Serves 8

Beef Shepherd's Pie Topped with Garlic Mashed Potatoes

*N*o, this isn't the shepherd's pie you remember from the school cafeteria. Simple and straightforward, with a rich sauce and a tasty garlic mashed potato crust, this pie replaces the ground lamb or beef with tender chunks of beef. Served with a crisp green salad and a red wine, this is a wonderful company dinner.

$^{1}/_{4}$ cup flour

2 teaspoons salt, or to taste

$^{3}/_{4}$ teaspoon freshly ground black pepper, or to taste

$2^{1}/_{2}$ pounds beef stew meat, cut into 1-inch chunks

2 tablespoons olive oil

4 cups beef broth

1 teaspoon dried thyme

1 bay leaf

1 recipe Garlic Mashed Potatoes (recipe follows)

In a paper or plastic bag, combine the flour, 1 teaspoon of salt, and $^{1}/_{4}$ teaspoon of pepper, and dredge the beef in the coating, shaking off any excess. In a 5-quart Dutch oven or ovenproof casserole, heat the oil, adding the beef a few pieces at a time, browning it on all sides, about 8–10 minutes. When all the meat is browned, add the beef broth, thyme, and bay leaf. Simmer the stew, uncovered, for 45 minutes to 1 hour, or until the beef is tender.

Spread the potatoes over the beef in the casserole, dot them with the remaining teaspoon of butter, and bake in the preheated oven for 30 minutes, until the potatoes are golden brown.

Garlic Mashed Potatoes

2½ pounds red potatoes, cut into 1-inch chunks

1 teaspoon salt

4 cloves garlic

4 tablespoons butter, cut into bits

⅓ cup heavy cream

½ teaspoon freshly ground black or white pepper

Place the potatoes, garlic, and salt in a 3-quart saucepan with water to cover. Simmer the potatoes for 15 to 20 minutes, or until they are tender when pierced with a sharp knife. Drain the potatoes and garlic in a colander and return them to the pan, shaking them over the heat to dry them. Add 3½ tablespoons butter to the potatoes and mash the potatoes. Add the heavy cream and pepper, stirring to blend. Preheat the oven to 350° F.

Serves 6 to 8

Black Bean Sirloin Chili Topped with Jalapeño Corn Bread Crust

I'm sure you all have a favorite chili recipe, but I guarantee that this one will be a nice addition to your collection. Spicy and hearty with sirloin chunks, it is covered with a creamy corn bread studded with jalapeño peppers. Although this is not a five-alarm chili, if you would like yours with a little less heat, add the cayenne and jalapeños to taste.

CHILI

2 tablespoons olive oil

2 pounds boneless sirloin, cut into $1/2$-inch cubes

2 teaspoons salt

$1/2$ teaspoon freshly ground black pepper

2 cups chopped onions

6 cloves garlic, minced

4 fresh jalapeño peppers, seeded and finely chopped

$1/3$ cup masa harina

$1/4$ cup chili powder

$1/2$ teaspoon cayenne

$1/2$ teaspoon ground cumin

4 cups beef broth

2 cups cooked black beans

1 recipe Jalapeño Corn Bread Crust (see below)

In a heavy 5-quart Dutch oven, heat the oil over high heat. Sprinkle the meat with salt and pepper, and brown it in batches, transferring it to a bowl with a slotted spoon as it is done, about 8–10 minutes. In the fat remaining, cook the onions, garlic, and jalapeño peppers over moderate heat, stirring until the onion is softened, about 3–5 minutes. Add the masa harina, chili powder, cayenne, and cumin. Cook the mixture over medium heat for 5 minutes.

Gradually stir in the broth and browned beef, simmering the mixture uncovered, stirring occasionally, for 45 minutes. Stir in the beans. Transfer the chili to a 13 by 9-inch baking dish.

Preheat the oven to 375° F. Make the crust.

Bake the chili in the preheated oven for 30 minutes, or until the corn bread is golden brown and a toothpick inserted into the middle comes out clean.

Jalapeño Corn Bread Crust

1 1/2 cups yellow cornmeal

1/2 cup all-purpose flour

1 tablespoon sugar

2 teaspoons salt

2 tablespoons baking powder

1 egg

3/4 cup milk

2 tablespoons melted butter

1 (8-ounce) can cream-style corn

4 roasted jalapeño peppers, peeled, seeded, and chopped

1 cup freshly grated Cheddar cheese

In a large bowl, stir together the dry ingredients. Beat in the egg, milk, and butter. Fold in the corn, chopped peppers, and cheese. Pour the batter over the chili.

Serves 6 to 8

Broccoli Beef with Soba Noodle Pancake

A quick stir-fry of beef and broccoli with oyster sauce is topped with soba noodles, making a colorful statement that's ready in less than half an hour. Partially freezing the beef makes it easier to slice.

NOODLE PANCAKE
1 tablespoon vegetable oil
1 tablespoon sesame oil
8 ounces fresh soba noodles

BROCCOLI BEEF WITH OYSTER SAUCE
1 pound beef sirloin or flank, partially frozen, sliced paper thin against the grain
2 tablespoons soy sauce
2 cloves garlic, minced
2 teaspoons minced fresh ginger
2 tablespoons vegetable oil
$^1/_3$ cup chicken broth
2 teaspoons cornstarch
2 cups broccoli florets
2 tablespoons oyster sauce
$^1/_2$ cup chopped green onions

In a nonstick frying pan or wok over medium-high heat, heat the oils. Add the noodles and spread them out in the pan. Brown the noodles, on one side, and turn the pancake with a spatula to brown the other side, about 3 minutes each side. Remove the pancake from the pan, drain on paper towels, and keep it warm in a low oven.

Place the beef in a glass bowl. Stir in the soy sauce, 1 clove of garlic, 1 teaspoon of ginger, and 1 tablespoon of vegetable oil. Refrigerate the beef for 30 minutes.

Combine the broth and cornstarch in a small bowl and set it aside. In a wok, heat the remaining vegetable oil, add the remaining garlic and ginger, and the broccoli, and stir-fry for 2 minutes. Remove the broccoli from the wok and set it aside. Drain the beef from the marinade and add it to the hot wok. Stir-fry until the beef loses its pink color, about 2–3 minutes. Return the broccoli to the pan and add the oyster sauce, tossing to coat the broccoli and beef. Add the reserved broth and cornstarch to the pan, and stir until the sauce is thickened, about 2 minutes. Remove the wok from the heat, top the beef with the noodle pancake, and garnish with the chopped green onions.

Serves 6 to 8

Mom's Beef Stew Topped with
Sage Parmesan Biscuits

Beef pot pies were the stuff of '50s legend. Hearty beef simmered in a rich gravy, peeking out from under a short pastry crust. Most of the time, Mom would serve biscuits or rolls with dinner, but here I've topped the pie itself with cheesy herbed biscuits. The biscuits are wonderful all by themselves, but they make this pie ethereal. If you have a Crock-Pot, toss in all the ingredients and let the stew simmer for 6 hours, then transfer it to a 3-quart casserole to bake the biscuits.

BEEF STEW

2 pounds beef stew meat, cut into 1-inch chunks

1 teaspoon salt

$1/2$ teaspoon freshly ground black pepper

2 cloves garlic, mashed

1 tablespoon olive oil

3 cups beef broth

2 teaspoons chopped fresh sage, or 1 teaspoon dried

3 carrots, cut into 1-inch chunks

2 cups 1-inch potato cubes

1 cup fresh, or frozen and defrosted corn kernels

1 cup fresh or frozen and defrosted petite peas

1 recipe Sage Parmesan Biscuits (see below)

Sprinkle the beef with the salt, pepper, and garlic. In a 3-quart ovenproof casserole or Dutch oven, heat the oil. Add the meat, browning it on all sides for 6 to 8 minutes. When the meat is browned, add the broth, stirring to scrape up any bits that have stuck to the bottom of the pan. Add the sage, carrots, and potato cubes, cover, and simmer for 35 minutes. Add the corn and peas and continue to cook for another 10 to 15 minutes. The sauce will appear thin, but it will thicken when the biscuits bake. (The stew can be refrigerated at this point for 2 to 3 days, or frozen for up to 2 months.)

Make the biscuits. Bake the stew in the preheated oven for 17 to 20 minutes, or until the biscuits are browned and the stew is bubbling.

Sage Parmesan Biscuits

2 cups Bisquick
$^1/_2$ cup freshly grated Parmesan cheese
$^2/_3$ cup milk
1 teaspoon dried sage

Preheat the oven to 375° F. In a large mixing bowl, combine the Bisquick and Parmesan cheese. Add the milk and sage, stirring with a fork to combine. Turn the dough out onto a floured board and knead it 5 times. Roll the dough out to $^1/_2$ inch thick, and cut out individual biscuits with a 2-inch cutter, or transfer the entire crust to the top of the stew, cutting it to fit.

Serves 6 to 8

Steak and Ale Pie with Yorkshire Pudding Crust

*L*ondon broil cooked in dark ale with earthy Portobello mushrooms, then topped with a Yorkshire pudding crust, literally rises to great heights in a very hot oven. The steak and ale benefit from being made ahead of time, allowing the flavors to get to know one another. Make the Yorkshire pudding batter in advance and refrigerate it, then blend in the egg whites just before you are ready to bake it.

STEAK AND ALE FILLING

$1/4$ cup all-purpose flour

$1/2$ teaspoon salt

$1/8$ teaspoon freshly ground black pepper

2 pounds beef sirloin, trimmed of fat and cut into $1 1/2$-inch pieces

2 tablespoons olive oil

1 large onion, sliced $1/4$ inch thick

2 cloves garlic, minced

6 ounces (about 3) Portobello mushrooms, sliced $1/2$ inch thick

1 cup dark ale

3 cups beef broth

1 teaspoon dried sage

1 recipe Yorkshire Pudding Crust (see below)

Preheat the oven to 350° F.

In a mixing bowl or Ziploc bag, combine the flour, salt, and pepper. Add the beef a few pieces at a time, making sure that the meat is coated on all sides with the flour. In a 5-quart Dutch oven, heat the oil, add the meat, a few pieces at a time, and brown it on all sides, about 8–10 minutes. When all the meat is browned, add the onion and garlic, and sauté for 2 minutes. Add the mushrooms and continue to sauté for 5 minutes, until the onion is translucent and the mushrooms begin to give off some of their liquid. Add the ale, stirring to loosen any browned bits that are stuck to the bottom of the pan. Add the broth and sage, and bring the mixture to a boil.

Transfer the casserole to the preheated oven, and bake 45 minutes to 1 hour, until the meat is tender.

Make the crust. Preheat the oven to 425° F. Cover the hot stew with the pudding batter and bake for 15 minutes, then reduce the heat to 400° F. and bake for 10 to 15 minutes more.

Yorkshire Pudding Crust

2 eggs, plus 2 egg whites, stiffly beaten

1 teaspoon salt

1 cup all-purpose flour

1 cup milk

Place the whole eggs in a blender or food processor and pulse on and off 3 times. Add the salt, flour, and milk, and blend for 45 seconds. Refrigerate the batter for 45 minutes. When you are ready to bake, fold the egg whites into the batter. The crust will rise and be a golden brown.

Serves 6 to 8

Steak Pizzaiola with Herbed Focaccia Crust

*M*y *husband described this as an upside-down pizza, only better. The stew and focaccia dough can be prepared 2 days ahead and refrigerated, then assembled just before baking. The focaccia also makes a great side dish for another dinner. I've used oregano to flavor the focaccia, but feel free to substitute your own favorite herb.*

STEAK PIZZAIOLA FILLING
1 tablespoon olive oil

2 pounds beef round, cut into 1-inch chunks

1 teaspoon salt

$^1/_2$ teaspoon freshly ground black pepper

$^1/_2$ cup chopped onion

2 cloves garlic, minced

2 (16-ounce) cans chopped tomatoes in juice

$^1/_2$ teaspoon dried basil

2 tablespoons sugar

1 recipe Herbed Focaccia Crust (see below)

In a 5-quart Dutch oven or ovenproof casserole, heat the oil. Season the beef with the salt and the pepper, then add it to the hot pan and brown the meat on all sides. Add the onion and garlic, and sauté until the onion becomes translucent, about 2–3 minutes, being careful not to burn the garlic. Add the tomatoes, basil, and sugar to the pan, bringing the mixture to a boil. Stir the sauce, reduce the heat, and simmer, uncovered, for 35 to 45 minutes, until the meat is tender. (At this point, the stew may be refrigerated for 2 days, or frozen for up to 2 months.) While the steak is simmering, make the crust.

Preheat the oven to 400° F. Roll the dough out to fit your casserole dish. Place it over the stew, brush it with the remaining 2 tablespoons of olive oil, and sprinkle it with the remaining Parmesan cheese. Bake for 35 minutes, until the crust is golden brown. Cut into wedges and serve immediately.

Herbed Focaccia Crust

1¼ cups warm water (105° F.)

2 teaspoons active dry yeast

1 teaspoon sugar

1 teaspoon salt

5 tablespoons extra virgin olive oil

3 cups flour

6 tablespoons freshly grated Parmesan cheese

1 teaspoon dried oregano

In a glass measuring cup, sprinkle the yeast over the warm water. Add the sugar, and allow the yeast to proof. The yeast will begin to bubble after 10 minutes. If the yeast doesn't bubble, throw it away and start over again. Place the flour and 4 tablespoons of Parmesan cheese in a large mixing bowl. Gradually add the yeast, 2 tablespoons of the olive oil, and the oregano, stirring with a wooden spoon. When the dough forms a ball, turn it out onto a floured board and knead it 4 or 5 times. Place the dough ball in a greased mixing bowl, cover with a clean dish towel, and set it in a turned-off oven or microwave to rise for 45 minutes. (If you plan to make the focaccia later, brush with some additional olive oil and refrigerate the dough in a Ziploc bag.)

Serves 6

Tostada Grande Pie

*T*his pie has a cold "crust" of lettuce, tomatoes, and other ingredients. The pie itself is baked, then topped with the salad when it comes out of the oven. I have used ground beef, but if you would like to use ground turkey or chicken strips, sauté those first and add them to the pie. Present this as a buffet dish and serve the toppings on the side so that your guests can build their own pie. If you love spicy food, add 1 teaspoon cayenne to the ground beef mixture.

1½ pounds ground lean beef

1 large onion, chopped

2 teaspoons chili powder

½ teaspoon ground cumin

1 cup tomato puree

1 (15-ounce) can refried beans

2 cups freshly grated Colby cheese

1 cup freshly grated Monterey Jack cheese

2 cups shredded lettuce

1 cup chopped fresh tomato

½ cup chopped red onion

1 (4-ounce can) sliced ripe olives

¼ cup pickled sliced jalapeño peppers, drained

1 large avocado, diced, tossed with 1 teaspoon lemon juice

1 cup sour cream

4 cups assorted yellow, white, and blue corn tortilla chips

Preheat the oven to 375° F. Spray a 13 by 9-inch casserole with non-stick cooking spray. In a 12-inch skillet, sauté the ground beef until it loses its red color. Drain any fat that has accumulated in the pan, add the onion, chili powder, and cumin, and sauté until the onion turns translucent, about 4–5 minutes. Add the tomato puree, and bring to a boil.

Mash the refried beans and spread them in the bottom of the prepared pan. Sprinkle the beans with $^1/_2$ cup of the Colby cheese, top with the beef mixture and the remaining cheeses. (If you plan to serve this later, refrigerate it until ready to bake.) Place the pan in the preheated oven, and bake for 15 minutes, until the cheese is melted and bubbly. Remove the pan from the oven and top the pie with the remaining ingredients, in the order listed. Tuck the tortilla chips around the casserole and serve immediately.

Serves 6 to 8

Creole Sausage and Rice Pie with Red Bean Crust

Hearty, stick-to-your-ribs fare like this is wonderful on a cold evening, or for eating while you watch your favorite teams slug it out on the gridiron. The sausage and rice mixture cooks halfway before adding the crust of savory red beans. That way the beans don't sink to the bottom of the pot! The red beans can be made three days in advance, and the pie can be baked, then refrigerated for 2 days, and reheated, covered, in a low oven, or microwaved.

Cajun Sausage and Rice

1 tablespoon vegetable oil

2 pounds andouille or smoked Polish-type sausage, cut into $^1/_2$-inch rounds

1 cup chopped onion

1 cup chopped celery

2 cloves garlic, minced

1 cup chopped green bell pepper

1 teaspoon cayenne

$^1/_2$ teaspoon salt

$1^1/_2$ cups long-grain rice

$3^3/_4$ cups chicken broth

1 recipe Red Bean Crust (see below)

Chopped green onion, for garnish

Preheat the oven to 375° F. In a 12-inch sauté pan, heat the oil. Add the sausage, and sauté for 2 minutes. Add the onion, celery, garlic, green pepper, cayenne, and salt, and sauté for 4 to 5 minutes, until the onion begins to turn golden. Add the rice, and stir to coat it evenly. Gradually add the chicken broth, stirring up any browned bits from the bottom of the pan.

Transfer the rice mixture to a 13 by 9-inch casserole dish or a 4-quart casserole, and bake for 15 minutes. Make the Red Bean Crust.

At the end of 15 minutes, the rice should have absorbed most of the liquid. Carefully spoon the Red Bean Crust over the top of the rice. Bake for another 10 minutes, until the rice is tender. Garnish the casserole with the chopped green onion.

Red Bean Crust

1 tablespoon olive oil

1 cup chopped onions

$^1/_2$ cup chopped celery

$^1/_2$ cup chopped red or green bell pepper

3 cloves garlic, minced

4 cups canned red beans, drained and rinsed

1 teaspoon salt

$^1/_2$ teaspoon freshly ground black pepper

1 bay leaf

$^1/_2$ cup chicken broth

Heat the oil in a 4-quart saucepan. Add the onion, celery, chopped pepper, and garlic and sauté, until the onion is translucent, about 4 minutes. Add the beans, salt, pepper, and bay leaf, stirring to combine. Slowly pour in the broth, and simmer for 30 minutes. (Refrigerate the beans until ready to proceed.)

Serves 6 to 8

Cider Braised Pork Pie with Sweet Potato Crust

*T*he smell of this pot pie made all of my tasters salivate. The combination of pork and apples perfumed the house, and the mashed sweet potato crust with crunchy pecans was the perfect complement to this dinner.

Cider Braised Pork

$^1/_2$ cup all-purpose flour

1 teaspoon salt

$^1/_4$ teaspoon freshly ground black pepper

$^1/_4$ teaspoon ground ginger

6 (1$^1/_2$-inch-thick) boneless loin pork chops

1 tablespoon vegetable oil

3 Granny Smith Apples, peeled, cored, and sliced $^1/_2$-inch thick

1$^1/_2$ cups apple cider

$^1/_2$ cup beef broth

1 cup chicken broth

1 recipe Sweet Potato Crust (see below)

$^1/_2$ cup chopped pecans

2 tablespoons butter, cut into slivers

In a mixing bowl or on a flat plate, combine the flour, salt, pepper, and ginger. Dredge the pork chops in the mixture and set them aside. In a 5-quart Dutch oven, heat the oil and brown the pork chops on both sides. Add the apples to the pan and cook for 2 to 3 minutes, until the apples begin to soften. Add the cider and broth, stirring to loosen any browned bits that may be stuck to the bottom of the pan.

Reduce the heat and simmer partially covered for 45 minutes until the pork chops are tender. Make the Sweet Potato Crust. At the end of the cooking time, remove the pork chops and apples from the sauce with a slotted spoon and arrange them in an ovenproof baking dish. (I use a 12-inch round, 2-inch deep casserole dish.) Stirring with a whisk, reduce the sauce over medium-high for about 10 minutes, until it thickens. Pour 1 cup of the sauce into the casserole dish, and save the rest for serving alongside the finished pie. Spread the Sweet Potato Crust over the pork chops in the casserole dish. Dot the top with butter, sprinkle with pecans, and bake in a preheated 375° F. oven for 15 minutes, until the top is golden brown. Serve immediately with additional sauce on the side.

Sweet Potato Crust
4 sweet potatoes (about 3 pounds)
¼ cup light brown sugar
1 teaspoon salt
3 tablespoons softened butter

Preheat the oven to 450° F. Scrub the potatoes, and prick them several times with the point of a sharp knife. Bake the sweet potatoes for 1 hour, or until they are soft when squeezed. Peel the potatoes, and place the flesh in a mixing bowl. Add the brown sugar and salt, mashing the potatoes until they are smooth. Add the butter, a tablespoon at a time, to make a stiff but smooth mixture. (The potatoes may be refrigerated until you are ready to use them. Rewarm them in a double boiler over simmering water, or in the microwave.)

Serves 6

Ham Pot Pie Topped with Scalloped Potato Gratin

*T*his pie is a perfect way to use up leftover ham. It's a great dish for brunch, or a Sunday dinner, and it can be made a day ahead. Serve it with fruit, or a fruit and vegetable salad, on the side.

5 medium red potatoes, sliced $1/4$ inch thick

$1^1/2$ teaspoons salt

$1/2$ teaspoon freshly ground black pepper

1 small onion, cut into $1/2$-inch slices

$1/3$ pound ham, sliced very thin, or julienne strips of thicker ham slices

$2^1/2$ cups heavy cream

3 eggs

1 tablespoon Dijon mustard

2 cups freshly grated Swiss cheese

Preheat the oven to 400° F. Butter a 13 by 9-inch baking pan. Spread a layer of potatoes on the bottom of the pan, and sprinkle the potatoes with some of the salt and pepper. Cover the potatoes with a few of the onion slices, a layer of ham, and then another layer of potatoes. Season and continue the layering process until you have used all the potatoes for the final layer.

In a bowl, beat together the cream, eggs, and mustard. Pour the mixture over the potatoes, and sprinkle the top with the grated cheese. (The pie may be refrigerated overnight at this point before serving. Bring it to room temperature before baking.)

When ready to bake, cover the casserole with aluminum foil and bake it for 30 minutes. Uncover and bake for an additional 30 minutes, until the potatoes are tender, and the cheese is golden. Serve immediately.

Serves 6 to 8

Pork Loin Pie with Braised Sauerkraut and Caramelized Onion Crust

Hearty and robust, this pie would be the perfect centerpiece for an Oktoberfest celebration. Don't be put off by the number of onions, they will reduce and become a sweet and delicious topping for this pie. We love it with mashed potatoes and applesauce on the side.

³/₄ cup brown sugar

¹/₄ cup Dijon mustard

2 pounds boneless pork loin, cut into 1-inch chunks

1¹/₂ cups beef broth

4 cups sauerkraut, rinsed and drained

4 tablespoons butter

6 cups ¹/₂-inch-thick onion slices

In a small bowl, combine ¹/₂ cup of the brown sugar and the Dijon mustard. Coat the pork with the mixture, and sauté it in a 5-quart Dutch oven over medium-high heat, until browned, about 8–10 minutes. When the meat is browned, add the beef broth to the casserole, then cover the pork with the sauerkraut. Simmer the mixture, covered, over medium-low heat for 30 minutes.

In a large sauté pan, melt the butter, add the onions, and sauté over medium-high heat, stirring constantly, for 15 to 20 minutes. Sprinkle the onions with the remaining ¹/₄ cup of brown sugar, and continue to cook until the onions have caramelized and are tender, being careful not to burn them. When the onions are ready, spread them over the pork and sauerkraut. Simmer the pork, uncovered, for another 10 minutes, or until the meat is tender. (The finished pie can be refrigerated for 2 days; bring it back to a simmer, and reheat for 15 to 20 minutes.) Reheat, uncovered, on the stove top.

Serves 6 to 8

Pork Tamale Pie with Southwestern Crust

*T*amale pie is another standard of school cafeterias and Mom's kitchen that may have given Mexican food a bad name. This tamale pie substitutes tender chunks of pork for ground meat, and cooks in a spicy, sweet, cumin-flavored sauce. The topping is a cheesy cornbread crust instead of the traditional cornmeal mush.

TAMALE FILLING

1 tablespoon vegetable oil

1 teaspoon salt

$^1/_2$ teaspoon freshly ground black pepper

2 pounds boneless pork loin, trimmed of fat, cut into 1$^1/_2$-inch cubes

2 cloves garlic, minced

1 cup finely chopped onion

$^1/_2$ cup chopped Anaheim chile peppers (mild)

$^1/_2$ teaspoon ground cumin

2 teaspoons chili powder

3 cups canned chopped tomatoes

2 tablespoons sugar

2 cups fresh, or frozen and defrosted corn kernels

1 recipe Cornmeal Crust (see below)

In a 5-quart Dutch oven, heat the vegetable oil. Sprinkle the pork with the salt and pepper, and add it to the pan. Brown the pork on all sides, turning it frequently. When the meat is browned, about 6–8 minutes, add the garlic, onion, and Anaheim chilies. Stir the vegetables and add the cumin and chili powder. Sauté the vegetables for about 4 minutes, until the onion starts to become translucent. Add the tomatoes, stirring up any browned bits that have accumulated on the bottom of the pan. Add the sugar and corn, bringing the mixture to a boil. Reduce the heat and simmer, partially covered, for 30 to 45 minutes, until the pork is tender. Transfer the tamale filling to an ovenproof baking dish.

Preheat the oven to 375° F. Make the crust. Spoon the mixture over the tamale filling and bake for 35 to 45 minutes, until the corn bread is browned and a toothpick inserted in the center comes out clean.

Cornmeal Crust

1 cup yellow cornmeal

2 tablespoons sugar

1 cup all-purpose flour

1 tablespoon baking powder

2 tablespoons melted butter

$3/4$ cup milk

1 egg

1 cup freshly grated Colby or mild Cheddar cheese

6 shakes Tabasco sauce

In a large mixing bowl, combine the cornmeal, sugar, flour, and baking powder, whisking to aerate the flour. Blend in the butter, milk, and egg, stirring until the batter is smooth. Fold in the cheese and Tabasco.

Serves 6 to 8

Pork with Mango Ginger Sauce
Topped with Curried Phyllo

*T*ropical mango and chunks of pork tenderloin combine under crispy curry-flavored phyllo to make a delightful pie. The pie can be assembled 2 days ahead of time.

PORK FILLING
1 tablespoon vegetable oil

1 teaspoon salt

$^1/_2$ teaspoon freshly ground black pepper

1 teaspoon chopped fresh ginger

1 clove garlic, minced

2 pork tenderloins (approximately $1^1/_2$ pounds, $^3/_4$ lb. each), cut into 1-inch chunks

1 (8-ounce) can mango nectar

1 cup chicken broth

1 mango, peeled and cut into $^1/_2$-inch dice

1 recipe Curried Phyllo Crust (see below)

In a 5-quart Dutch oven, heat the oil. Make a paste of the salt, pepper, ginger, and garlic. Rub the pork with the paste, and brown the pork on all sides, for 6 to 8 minutes. When the pork is browned, add the mango nectar and chicken broth to the pan, scraping up any browned bits from the bottom. Cover the pan and simmer for 30 minutes. At the end of the cooking time, stir in the mango. Transfer the pork mixture to an ovenproof baking dish. Make the crust.

Preheat the oven to 400° F. Bake the pie for 30 to 35 minutes, until the crust is golden.

Curried Phyllo Crust

6 sheets phyllo dough, defrosted

½ cup melted butter

½ teaspoon curry powder

½ cup dry bread crumbs

Cover the sheets of phyllo with a clean kitchen towel. Stir the curry powder into the butter. Remove 1 sheet of phyllo and brush it all over with the curry-butter mixture. Sprinkle the phyllo with some of the dry bread crumbs, and lay it on top of the pork in the baking dish. Repeat the process with the remaining phyllo, but do not sprinkle the last sheet with bread crumbs. Tuck the phyllo in around the sides of the dish. (At this point, you may refrigerate the entire pie for 2 days.)

Serves 8

Tuscan Braised Pork with Polenta Crust

*P*olenta, *that creamy cornmeal side dish, serves as the crust for a robust pork pot pie that simmers in a wine and tomato sauce thick with vegetables. Instant polenta works well here, and cooks in half the time.*

PORK FILLING

2 tablespoons olive oil

2 pounds lean pork, cut into 1-inch cubes

1$\frac{1}{2}$ teaspoons salt

$\frac{1}{2}$ teaspoon freshly ground black pepper

1 cup chopped onion

3 medium carrots, cut into $\frac{1}{2}$-inch rounds

3 stalks celery, cut into $\frac{1}{2}$-inch slices

1 cup red wine

3 cups chopped tomatoes (two 15$\frac{1}{2}$-ounce cans)

1$\frac{1}{2}$ teaspoons coarsely chopped fresh sage, or $\frac{3}{4}$ teaspoon dried

1 recipe Polenta Crust (see below)

Preheat the oven to 350° F. In a 5-quart Dutch oven, heat the oil. Sprinkle the pork with the salt and pepper and add it to the pot, a few pieces at a time, browning it on all sides, about 6–8 minutes. When all the pork is browned, add the onion, carrots, and celery, and sauté the vegetables for 5 minutes. Add the wine, and allow it to boil for 2 minutes. Add the tomatoes and sage, stirring up any browned bits that may be stuck to the bottom of the pan. Cover and bake in the preheated oven for 30 minutes.

Meanwhile, make the crust. Bake for an additional 15 minutes, until the polenta is firm and the cheese is melted. Serve immediately.

Polenta Crust

4 cups water

1 teaspoon salt

1 cup instant polenta

3 tablespoons softened butter

¼ cup freshly grated Parmesan cheese

2 tablespoons chopped fresh flat-leaf parsley

In a 3-quart saucepan, bring the water and salt to a boil. Add the polenta, whisking until it is smooth. Cook the polenta, stirring it with a wooden spoon, for about 15 minutes. Remove it from the heat and stir in the butter. Spread the polenta over the pork and sprinkle it evenly with the cheese and parsley.

Serves 6 to 8

Lamb Pie with Goat Cheese Mashed Potato Crust

*G*oat cheese beaten into mashed potatoes makes a crust you will not forget. Tangy and creamy, it's a great covering for the savory lamb stew that bubbles beneath. The lamb can be made 2 days ahead and refrigerated, and the potatoes can be made a day ahead. Put them together just before baking. For a different twist, try using an herbed goat cheese for the potatoes.

LAMB FILLING

2 tablespoons olive oil

$^1/_4$ cup all-purpose flour

1$^1/_2$ teaspoons salt

$^1/_2$ teaspoon freshly ground black pepper

2 pounds boneless lamb, cut into 1-inch cubes

1 cup $^1/_2$-inch-thick onion slices

3 cloves garlic

1 cup red wine

2 cups chicken broth

1$^1/_2$ teaspoons dried thyme

1 bay leaf

1 recipe Goat Cheese Mashed Potato Crust (see below)

2 tablespoons butter

Preheat the oven to 350° F.

In a 5-quart Dutch oven, heat the oil. In a small bowl, combine the flour, salt, and pepper. Toss the lamb cubes in the mixture, then brown the meat in the hot oil, a few pieces at a time. When all the lamb is browned, about 6–8 minutes, add the onion and garlic, and sauté until the vegetables are soft, about 3–4 minutes. Pour in the wine, and scrape up any browned bits that may be stuck to the bottom of the pan. Add the broth, thyme, and bay leaf, stirring the sauce. Cover the pan, and bake in the preheated oven for 30 minutes.

Make the crust. Remove the bay leaf from the lamb stew. Spread the potatoes over the stew and dot the top with butter. Bake uncovered for an additional 20 minutes, until the potatoes are golden.

Goat Cheese Mashed Potato Crust
4 cups mashed potatoes
1 (5-ounce) container goat cheese
2 to 4 tablespoons milk

Place the potatoes in a mixing bowl and beat in the goat cheese, thinning the mixture with the milk.

Serves 8

Pot Roasted Lamb with Rosemary White Bean Crust

*L*amb *and rosemary are a match made in culinary heaven. The robust flavor of the lamb takes on the strong scent of the rosemary as the white beans float on top of the broth to provide a creamy crust for the pie. This pie actually improves with age, so make it a day or two ahead and reheat it in the oven before serving.*

2 tablespoons olive oil

3 pounds boneless lamb, cut into 1$\frac{1}{2}$-inch cubes

2 teaspoons salt

1 teaspoon freshly ground black pepper

3 cloves garlic, minced

1$\frac{1}{2}$ cups finely chopped onions

1 cup finely chopped carrots

1 cup finely chopped celery

1 tablespoon dried rosemary

2 tablespoons flour

3 cups chicken broth

2 cups beef broth

4 cups cooked white beans

2 cups dry bread crumbs

$\frac{1}{4}$ cup chopped fresh flat-leaf parsley

Preheat the oven to 375° F. In a 5-quart Dutch oven, heat the oil. Sprinkle the lamb with the salt and pepper, and brown it in the hot oil a few pieces at a time, removing the pieces from the pan as they are done, about 6–8 minutes. Add the garlic, onions, carrots, celery, and 2 teaspoons of the rosemary to the pan, and sauté for 3 minutes, until the vegetables begin to soften. Stir in the flour and cook for 3 minutes, until the flour begins to bubble, then gradually whisk in the broths, bringing the liquid to a boil.

Return the lamb to the pan and simmer for 10 minutes. Float the beans on top of the pie. In a bowl, combine the bread crumbs, the remaining teaspoon of rosemary, and the parsley, and sprinkle the mixture on top of the beans. Bake the pie for 45 minutes to 1 hour, until the crust is browned and the meat is tender.

Serves 6 to 8

Mediterranean Lamb Stew Topped with Eggplant Soufflé

*L*amb and eggplant pair beautifully in this robust main dish. The richness of the lamb and the sauce are absorbed into the soufflé-like topping.

LAMB STEW

1/2 cup all-purpose flour

1 teaspoon salt

1/2 teaspoon freshly ground black pepper

2 cloves garlic, crushed

2 pounds boneless lamb, cut into 2-inch cubes

2 tablespoons olive oil

1 large onion, sliced

1/2 cup dry red wine

1 1/4 cups beef broth

1 1/2 cups chicken broth

1 bay leaf

2 teaspoons crumbled dried rosemary

1 recipe Eggplant Soufflé (see below)

In a plastic bag, combine the flour, salt, pepper, and garlic, stirring to mix. Add the cubes of lamb and shake the bag to coat the meat. In a 5-quart Dutch oven heat the olive oil and add the lamb a few pieces at a time, shaking the pan to brown the lamb on all sides, about 8–10 minutes. When all the lamb is browned, add the onion and continue to cook over medium heat until the onion is translucent, about 4–5 minutes. Deglaze the pan with the wine, scraping up the browned bits from the bottom of the pan. Add the broth, bringing the mixture to a boil. Add the bay leaf and rosemary, reduce the heat to a simmer, and partially cover the pan. Cook for 45 minutes to 1 hour, until the meat is tender.

Meanwhile, prepare the eggplant soufflé. When ready to serve, spoon the eggplant over the lamb stew. Bake at 400° F. for 10 to 25 minutes, or until set. Serve immediately.

Eggplant Soufflé

This savory soufflé is an excellent complement to the lamb stew, and can be made ahead of time and refrigerated. It is also delicious served with grilled chicken or fish and topped with tomato salsa.

2 (1-pound) eggplants
Olive oil, as needed
4 cloves garlic
2 tablespoons butter
2 tablespoons flour
1 cup milk
$1/2$ teaspoon salt
$1/8$ teaspoon freshly ground black pepper
$1/4$ cup freshly grated Swiss cheese
1 egg
1 cup fresh bread crumbs

Preheat the oven to 375° F. Line a cookie sheet with aluminum foil. Cut the eggplants in half lengthwise, and brush the cut sides with olive oil. Place the eggplants cut side down, on the cookie sheet along with the garlic cloves, and bake for 45 minutes, or until the eggplants are tender. Allow them to cool for 10 minutes, then scoop out the insides of the eggplants, place the flesh in a food processor, or chop it coarsely. Squeeze the garlic out of its peel and add it to the eggplant.

recipe continues on following page

continued from previous page

In a saucepan, melt the butter, add the flour, and whisk over medium-high heat until the flour forms white bubbles. Gradually whisk in the milk, salt, and pepper, blending until the sauce is thickened, about 4–5 minutes. Remove the sauce from the heat and add the cheese, whisking until the cheese is melted. Beat the egg with a whisk and add it to the eggplant. Add the sauce and bread crumbs to the eggplant, and stir to blend. At this point, the soufflé can be refrigerated until ready to use.

Serves 6 to 8

Veal Osso Buco with Risotto Gremolata Crust

*S*ucculent veal simmers in a tomato and white wine sauce, then is covered with a risotto crust sprinkled with a zesty lemon and parsley garnish in this deliciously easy and comforting pie. An easy do-ahead buffet dish, all the elements can be prepared ahead of time and put together just before baking.

VEAL OSSO BUCO

1 tablespoon butter

1 tablespoon olive oil

2 pounds veal, cut into 1-inch chunks

1 onion, finely chopped

2 carrots, finely chopped

2 stalks celery, finely chopped

1 clove garlic, minced

1 teaspoon salt

$1/4$ teaspoon freshly ground black pepper

$1/3$ cup white wine

$1^{1}/_{2}$ cups chicken broth

1 cup beef broth

2 cups chopped tomatoes (either fresh or canned)

1 teaspoon dried thyme

1 recipe Risotto (see below)

2 tablespoons finely chopped fresh flat-leaf parsley

1 clove garlic, minced

1 tablespoon freshly grated lemon zest

In a 5-quart Dutch oven or ovenproof casserole, melt the butter with the olive oil. Add the veal and brown it on all sides, about 6–8 minutes. When the veal has browned, add the onion, carrots, celery, and garlic. Stir the mixture and cook until the onion is translucent, about 4–5 minutes. Add the salt and pep-

recipe continues on following page

continued from previous page

per, and deglaze the pan with the white wine. Stir the mixture, then loosen any browned bits that may have stuck to the bottom of the pan. Add the broths and the tomatoes, bringing the mixture to a boil. Stir in the thyme, reduce the heat, and simmer, partially covered, for 35 to 45 minutes, until the veal is tender. (At this point the stew can be refrigerated for 2 days, or frozen for 2 months.)

Make the crust.

When ready to assemble the pie, preheat the oven to 350° F. Pour the stew into a 13 by 9-inch casserole. Using the aluminum foil, turn the risotto onto the veal stew. In a small bowl, combine the parsley, garlic, and lemon zest. Sprinkle the top of the casserole with the mixture. Bake for 30 minutes, until the risotto is golden brown and the stew is bubbling.

Risotto

2 tablespoons butter
$^1/_4$ cup finely chopped onion
2 cups arborio rice
3 cups chicken broth
$^1/_2$ cup freshly grated Parmesan cheese

In a 3-quart saucepan, melt the butter. Add the onion and cook it for 3 minutes, until translucent. Add the rice, and cook it, stirring, for a minute or two, until the rice is coated with the butter. Add half of the broth, and stir the mixture over medium-high heat until all the broth is absorbed, about 8–12 minutes. Continue adding the broth, $^1/_2$ cup at a time, allowing each portion to be absorbed before adding more. At the end of the cooking time, about 25 minutes, stir in the grated cheese. Remove the rice from the heat. Allow to cool by spreading it into a 13 by 9-inch rectangle on a cookie sheet lined with aluminum foil.

Serves 8

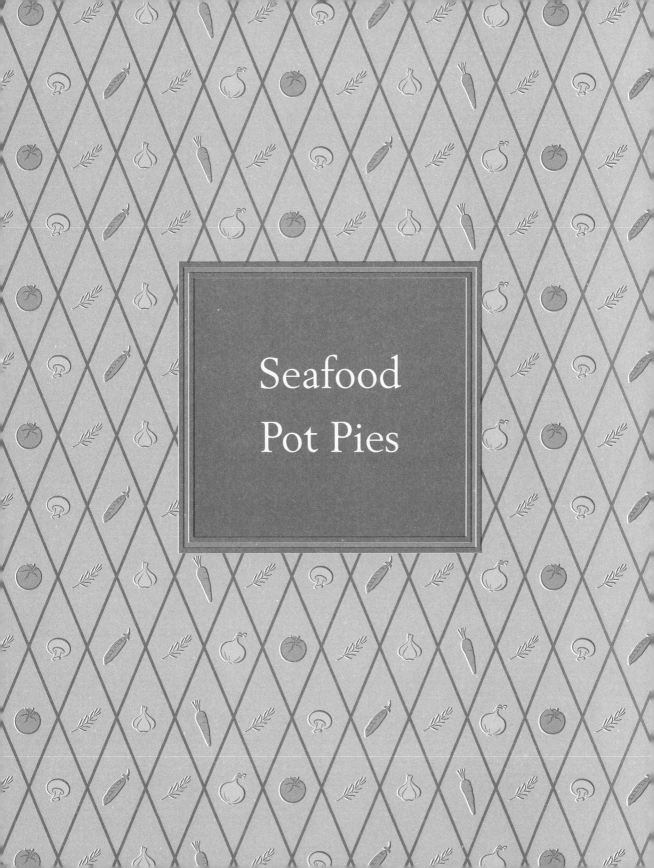

Seafood
Pot Pies

Halibut Pie with Cheddar Dill Biscuits

Mahi Mahi Pie with Tropical Fruit Salsa Crust

Monkfish Pie with Basil Pesto Crust

Snapper Veracruz with Jalapeño Jack Cheese Crust

Sole Pizzaiola Pie

Salmon Leek Pie with Lemon Dill Crust

Smoked Salmon Pie with Cornmeal Crust

Swiss Salmon Spinach Pie

Lobster Pie

Louisiana Crawfish Pie

Seafood Brunch Pie Topped with Crab Cake Crust

Seafood Pie with Shrimp Mashed Potato Crust

Seafood Ragout Moët & Chandon

Seafood Rockefeller Pot Pie

Shellfish Pie with Tarragon Artichoke Crust

Cajun Shrimp Pie with Creamy Corn Crust

Stuffed Shrimp Pie

Mediterranean Shrimp Pie with Feta Crust

Down East Clam Pie with Bacon Biscuit Crust

Mussel Bisque Pie

Sherried Scallop Pie with Parmesan Puff Pastry Crust

 ARLY cookbooks record fish pies as popular entrées. One in particular was called "Star Gazy," which featured a whole fish (sometimes an eel) with its head peeking through holes in the top crust. Mom wouldn't have surprised us with that creation, so we'll stick to fresh fish and shellfish covered with unique crusts. Fresh fish and shellfish make elegant and easy fare for pot pies. Although some of you may not be adventurous when it comes to fish, I recommend trying some of these recipes because fish and shellfish make some of the best meals. And if your seven year old says, "What's this?", you can reply, "Tastes like chicken!"

Fresh fish should be available at your local grocer or fish market. If you can't find a particular fish called for in one of these recipes, substitute something that is comparable, either a thin fish, or a thick, firm-fleshed fish. Since fresh fish is so moist, searing it before it goes into the pie helps to seal in the natural juices. Some shellfish, such as scallops, cook so quickly that they can be dropped raw into a hot sauce, covered, and cooked under the pastry cover.

I think seafood pies make wonderful statements for dinner, and I sometimes serve them for special occasions. I make an individual pie for each guest, so that they feel they have been given their own special present for dinner. It's amazing how much fun cooking can be when you surprise your family and friends.

Halibut Pie with Cheddar Dill Biscuits

*A*ny firm-fleshed fish can be used for this delicious pie, but we like halibut best. The halibut is pan seared, then baked in a garlicky lemon sauce, covered by a light-as-a-feather Cheddar dill biscuit crust. Depending upon the size of your baking dish, you may have a bit of the biscuit dough left over. If so, cut the dough into individual biscuits to serve alongside— you can never get enough of a good thing!

HALIBUT FILLING
1 tablespoon Creole Seasoning (page 8)
6 halibut fillets (1¹/₂ to 2 pounds total)
1 tablespoon olive oil
2 tablespoons plus ¹/₂ cup butter
6 cloves garlic, mashed
2 tablespoons freshly squeezed lemon juice

1 recipe Cheddar Dill Biscuits (see below)
2 tablespoons melted butter

Sprinkle both sides of the halibut fillets with the Creole seasoning. In a 10- or 12-inch sauté pan, heat the olive oil with 2 tablespoons of the butter. When the butter is melted and bubbling, brown the halibut on both sides, 3 minutes on each side. Remove the halibut to an ovenproof baking dish large enough to hold the fillets in one layer without crowding. Melt the remaining butter in the sauté pan, and sauté the garlic for 2 minutes until it is soft, but don't allow it to brown. Add the lemon juice to the pan, stirring to blend it with the butter. Pour the butter sauce over the halibut.

Preheat the oven to 375° F. Make the biscuit dough.

Cut the dough to fit the ovenproof dish, and lay it over the dish, covering the halibut fillets. Brush the top with the melted butter, and bake the pie in the preheated oven for 20 minutes, until the crust is golden brown. To serve, cut into

the crust, and serve each person 1 fillet topped with crust, spooning some of the pan juices over all.

Cheddar Dill Biscuits

Not all Cheddar is created equal when it comes to liquid content, so if the biscuits appear dry when you are kneading them, add additional heavy cream 1/2 teaspoon at a time, during the kneading process until you achieve the proper consistency.

3 cups flour
1 1/2 tablespoons baking powder
1 tablespoon sugar
2 1/4 teaspoons salt
2 cups heavy cream
1 cup freshly grated Cheddar cheese
2 tablespoons chopped fresh dillweed, or 1 tablespoon dried

In a large mixing bowl, whisk the flour, baking powder, sugar, and salt together. Make a well in the center of the dry ingredients and add the heavy cream, stirring with a fork to blend. Add the Cheddar cheese and dill, stirring until the mixture comes together. Turn the dough out onto a floured board, and knead it 4 to 5 times, until the flour and cheese are incorporated and the dough is smooth. If the dough does not come together, add some additional cream during the heating process. Roll the dough out 1/2 inch thick.

Serves 6

Mahi Mahi Pie with Tropical Fruit Salsa Crust

*C*runchy *with macadamia nuts, covered with a sweet, hot salsa, this pie will be one of your favorites. Make sure to refrigerate the breaded fish for a least 1 hour before sautéing, so that the breading will adhere to the fish. The salsa can be made 2 days ahead of time and kept in the refrigerator. If mangos are not in season, use cantaloupe or honeydew melon, adding more sugar as needed.*

1 recipe Tropical Fruit Salsa (see below)

MAHI MAHI PIE FILLING

2 eggs

$^1/_4$ cup water

2 teaspoons salt

$^1/_4$ teaspoon freshly ground black pepper

6 to 8 (6-ounce) Mahi Mahi fillets (or you can substitute red snapper)

$1^1/_2$ cups finely chopped macadamia nuts

2 cups dry bread crumbs

$^1/_2$ teaspoon ground ginger

2 tablespoons butter

2 tablespoons vegetable oil

Make the salsa and refrigerate.

In a mixing bowl, whisk together the eggs, water, 1 teaspoon of the salt, and the pepper. Add the fish fillets to the bowl, and stir until the fish is coated with the egg. On a flat plate, combine the nuts, bread crumbs, the remaining salt, and the ginger. Dredge 1 fillet at a time in the crumb mixture, turning to make sure both sides are evenly coated. Place the fillets on a plate after they are coated. Cover the plate with plastic wrap and refrigerate the fillets for at least 1 hour before frying.

When ready to serve, preheat the broiler and melt the butter and oil in a sauté pan. Sauté the fish until the fillets are crisp on both sides, about 3 minutes a side. Remove the fillets to a 13 by 9-inch baking dish. Cover the fish with the salsa, and set the dish under the broiler until the salsa begins to bubble and turn light gold, about 4–6 minutes. Serve immediately.

Tropical Fruit Salsa

2 cups chopped fresh mango

1 clove garlic, minced

$^1/_4$ cup chopped jalapeño pepper

2 tablespoons chopped fresh cilantro

1 teaspoon chopped fresh flat-leaf parsley

$^1/_4$ cup chopped green onions

$^1/_3$ cup sugar

4 shakes Tabasco sauce

1 teaspoon salt

2 tablespoons freshly squeezed lime juice

1 tablespoon rice wine vinegar

In a small glass mixing bowl, combine all the ingredients and stir until the sugar and salt have dissolved. Store in the refrigerator for at least 6 hours, stirring occasionally.

Serves 6

Monkfish Pie with Basil Pesto Crust

*M*onkfish is described as a poor man's lobster. Rich and succulent, it is stellar in this tomato cream sauce, covered with a pesto-flavored crust. The filling can be made ahead and refrigerated for 24 hours. The crust can be refrigerated overnight, or frozen for up to 1 month.

1 recipe Basil Pesto Crust (see below)

MONKFISH FILLING

1 tablespoon butter

1 tablespoon olive oil

$1/2$ cup chopped onion

$1/2$ cup chopped celery

1 teaspoon dried thyme

2 cups peeled, seeded, and chopped tomatoes

1 cup clam juice

$3/4$ cup white wine

$1/2$ teaspoon salt

$1/2$ teaspoon freshly ground black pepper

2 cups heavy cream

2 pounds monkfish fillets, cut into 1-inch pieces

$1/2$ pound rock shrimp, or medium shrimp, peeled and deveined

Prepare the crust and refrigerate.

Preheat the oven to 400° F. In a sauté pan, melt the butter with the oil. Add the onion, celery, and thyme, stirring until the onion is softened, about 3–4 minutes. Add the tomatoes, clam juice, wine, salt, and pepper. Simmer the mixture for 10 minutes, until it is reduced. Add the heavy cream and keep the sauce warm over low heat.

Divide the shrimp and monkfish among 8 individual ramekins, or arrange them in a 3-quart baking dish. Pour the sauce over the fish. Roll the dough out to fit the pie dish, cover the pie, and bake in the preheated oven for 25 to 35 minutes, until the crust is golden.

Basil Pesto Crust

1½ cups all-purpose flour
1 teaspoon salt
4 tablespoons butter, cut into ½-inch bits
2 tablespoons prepared basil pesto sauce
¼ cup ice cold water

Place the flour and salt in the work bowl of a food processor (see Note). Distribute the butter over the flour and pulse on and off 3 times. Add the pesto, and pulse again twice. With the machine running, add the water, 1 tablespoon at a time, until the dough begins to come together. Turn the dough out onto a floured board and knead it into a 6-inch disc. Wrap the disc in plastic wrap, and refrigerate it for 30 minutes.

NOTE: If you don't own a food processor, cut the butter into the flour with a pastry blender, or with your fingertips. Add the pesto and water, blending, until the crust begins to form a ball. Roll out as directed.

Serves 6 to 8

Snapper Veracruz with Jalapeño Jack Cheese Crust

Spicy green chilies and tomatoes liven up mild-flavored red snapper in this out-of-the-ordinary pie. Topped with a crumbly Jalapeño Jack Cheese Crust, it goes together quickly for a special dinner any day of the week. The sauce Veracruz may be prepared several days ahead of time and refrigerated until ready to bake. Try this technique with chicken, too.

1 tablespoon olive oil

2 Anaheim chili peppers, seeded and finely chopped

1/2 cup chopped onion

2 cloves garlic, mashed

1 teaspoon ground cumin

1 (16-ounce) can chopped tomatoes in puree

1 teaspoon freshly squeezed lime juice

1 1/2 teaspoons salt

1/2 teaspoon cayenne

8 red snapper fillets (4 to 6 ounces each)

1 recipe Jalapeño Jack Cheese Crust (see below)

In a sauté pan, heat the oil and add the chilies, onion, garlic, and cumin, stirring until the vegetables begin to soften, about 3–4 minutes. Add the tomatoes and lime juice, cooking until the mixture thickens. Season the sauce with 1 teaspoon of the salt, and 1/4 teaspoon of the cayenne. (Refrigerate until ready to bake.) Assemble the Jalapeño Jack Cheese Crust.

Preheat the oven to 375° F. Place the snapper fillets in a 13 by 9-inch baking dish or ovenproof casserole that will hold the fish in one layer. Season with the remaining salt and cayenne. Spread the Veracruz sauce evenly over the fillets, and top with the Jalapeño Jack Cheese Crust. Bake for 15 minutes, until the fish is cooked through and the crumbs are lightly browned.

Jalapeño Jack Cheese Crust

3 tablespoons butter
3 cups fresh French bread crumbs
8 ounces Jalapeño Pepper Jack cheese, grated
3 tablespoons chopped fresh cilantro

In a sauté pan, melt the butter, add the bread crumbs, and cook until the crumbs are toasted, about 3–5 minutes. Remove from the heat, place the crumbs in a bowl, and add the cheese and cilantro. Refrigerate until ready to use.

Serves 6 to 8

Sole Pizzaiola Pie

*E*veryone loves pizza, and this delicious pie is a great way to get your family to eat fish. Delicate sole fillets are topped with pizza sauce and cheese to produce a spectacular family-style meal in less than 45 minutes. The sauce can be made up ahead of time and refrigerated or frozen until ready to use. Serve this with crusty Italian bread and a green salad.

1 recipe Sauce Pizzaiola (see below)

SOLE
8 fillets of sole (about 1 pound)
$^1/_2$ teaspoon salt
$^1/_8$ teaspoon cayenne
2 cups freshly grated mozzarella cheese
1 tablespoon chopped fresh oregano

Make the sauce.

Preheat the oven to 400° F. Spray a 10-inch ovenproof dish with non-stick cooking spray. Sprinkle the fillets with salt and cayenne. Roll the fillets and place them in the baking dish (see Note). Cover them with the pizzaiola sauce. Sprinkle with the cheese and oregano. Bake for 10 minutes, until the cheese is melted and the sauce is bubbling. Serve immediately.

Sauce Pizzaiola

Fresh and quick, this will be a sauce that you'll make often. Keep some in the freezer to toss into pasta, or to use in another dinner.

2 tablespoons olive oil
$^1/_2$ cup chopped onion
1 clove garlic, minced
4 cups chopped fresh tomatoes
2 tablespoons chopped fresh basil
$1^1/_2$ teaspoons salt, plus additional to taste
$^1/_2$ teaspoon freshly ground black pepper, plus additional to taste

In a 3-quart saucepan, heat the olive oil. Add the onion and sauté for 2 minutes. Stir the garlic into the onion. Add the tomatoes, basil, $1^1/_2$ teaspoons salt, and $^1/_2$ teaspoon pepper, and bring the sauce to a simmer. Simmer uncovered for 30 minutes, or until the sauce has thickened. Taste, and adjust the seasoning with more salt and pepper. (Refrigerate for up to 2 days, or freeze for up to 2 months.)

NOTE: If you would like to serve individual pies, roll the fillets and place them in ramekins, cover with sauce, cheese, and oregano, and bake according to directions above.

Serves 6 to 8

Salmon Leek Pie with Lemon Dill Crust

*T*his savory pie has a gorgeous salmon pink filling and a crust flecked with green dill and lemon zest. The crust is easily made ahead of time, and the filling is a great way to use leftover cooked salmon.

1 recipe Lemon Dill Crust (see below)

SALMON LEEK FILLING
2 pounds salmon fillets
2 teaspoons Creole Seasoning (page 8)
2 tablespoons white wine
2 tablespoons butter
2 leeks, white part only, cut into $1/2$-inch slices
$1/2$ pound mushrooms, sliced
$1/2$ teaspoon salt
$1/4$ teaspoon Tabasco sauce
3 tablespoons flour
$1^1/2$ cups milk

Prepare the crust dough and refrigerate.

Preheat the oven to 400° F. Arrange the salmon in a microwave-safe dish with the Creole seasoning and white wine. Cover with plastic wrap and make 2 slits in the wrap to vent. Microwave on high for 6 minutes, until the salmon is cooked. (If you don't have a microwave, poach the salmon and seasoning with $1/2$ cup white wine and 2 tablespoons of butter in a 10-inch sauté pan.) Remove the salmon from the dish and cut it into 1-inch chunks. Set aside.

In a 10- to 12-inch sauté pan, heat the butter, add the leeks and mushrooms, and sauté for 3 minutes. Season with the salt and Tabasco. Sprinkle with the flour, and whisk until the flour begins to bubble. Gradually add the milk, and whisk until the sauce is smooth and thick, about 4 minutes. Remove from the heat, add the salmon, and transfer to a 10-inch ovenproof baking dish. Cover the pie with the lemon dill crust, slash 2 vents in the crust, and bake in the preheated oven for 35 minutes, until the crust is golden brown and the filling is bubbling.

Lemon Dill Crust

1½ cups all-purpose flour

½ teaspoon salt

1 tablespoon fresh dill weed

1 teaspoon freshly grated lemon zest

9 tablespoons butter, cut into ½-inch pieces

6 tablespoons ice water

Place the flour, salt, dill, and lemon zest in the work bowl of a food processor (see Note) and pulse on and off 3 times. Scatter the butter over the flour in the work bowl. Pulse on and off 4 times. Sprinkle 4 tablespoons of water over the flour and pulse on and off 4 times. When the dough begins to come together (looking crumbly, like a cobbler topping) turn it out onto a floured board and roll it into a 12-inch circle. If it doesn't come together, add the remaining water, pulsing, a few teaspoons at a time.

NOTE: If you don't have a food processor, place the flour, salt, dill, and zest in a large mixing bowl. Cut the butter into the flour with a pastry blender or your fingers. Add the water, a few tablespoons at a time, until the dough begins to come together. Continue as directed.

Serves 6

Smoked Salmon Pie with Cornmeal Crust

*S*moked salmon on cornmeal blini with sour cream and red onion is one of my favorite cocktail foods, and since you can never get enough of a good thing, I've translated that wonderful flavor into this delicious pie.

1 recipe Cornmeal Crust (see below)

SMOKED SALMON FILLING
8 ounces cream cheese, softened
$1/4$ cup sour cream
1 egg
1 tablespoon fresh dill weed
6 ($1/4$-inch-thick) slices red onion
6 ounces smoked salmon, thinly sliced, cut into $1/2$-inch strips

Make the crust and refrigerate. When ready to serve, preheat the oven to 375° F. Place the cornmeal crust on a cookie sheet lined with parchment or aluminum foil.

In a small mixing bowl, beat together the cream cheese, sour cream, egg, and dill. Spread the mixture over half the cornmeal crust. Top with the red onion and smoked salmon. Fold the crust over the filling and crimp the edges with a fork. Bake the pie for 20 minutes, until the crust is golden. Let the pie rest for 5 minutes before cutting it into wedges.

Cornmeal Crust

1 cup all-purpose flour

½ cup cornmeal

½ teaspoon salt

6 tablespoons cold vegetable shortening

4 to 6 tablespoons water

Place the flour, cornmeal, and salt in the work bowl of a food processor. Process on and off 3 times. Distribute the shortening over the flour mixture. Pulse the food processor on and off 3 times. With the machine running, add the water, a few tablespoons at a time, until the dough begins to come together. Turn the dough out onto a floured board and roll it into a 14-inch circle. Refrigerate.

NOTE: If you don't own a food processor, cut the shortening into the flour, cornmeal, and salt. Add the water a few tablespoons at a time, blending until the crust begins to form a ball. Roll out as directed.

Serves 6

Swiss Salmon Spinach Pie

*H*ere's an easy way to make salmon special. Try this unique topping on any thick-fleshed fish. It also works well with leftover chicken.

2 pounds salmon fillets

3 tablespoons butter

1 teaspoon Old Bay seasoning

2 tablespoons white wine

1 pound mushrooms, cleaned and sliced $1/2$ inch thick

2 (10-ounce) packages fresh baby spinach

$1/2$ teaspoon salt

$1/8$ teaspoon freshly ground black pepper

Pinch of freshly grated nutmeg

$1^1/2$ cups freshly grated Swiss cheese

Preheat the oven to 400° F. Using a sharp chef's knife, remove the skin from the salmon and discard. In a sauté pan over high heat, melt 2 tablespoons of butter. Sprinkle the salmon with the Old Bay seasoning, add the fillets to the hot pan, and sear quickly on both sides. Remove the salmon fillets from the pan and place them in a 13 by 9-inch baking dish. Add the wine and set the dish aside.

In a 10-inch sauté pan, melt the remaining butter. Add the mushrooms and sauté them for 2 to 3 minutes, then add the spinach. Toss the spinach with the mushrooms, and season with the salt, pepper, and nutmeg. When the spinach has wilted, spread the mixture over the salmon fillets. Sprinkle with the cheese, and bake for 10 to 15 minutes, or until the salmon is cooked through and the cheese is bubbly.

Serves 6

Lobster Pie

*L*uscious chunks of Maine lobster bathed in a smooth sherry bisque, then covered with buttery bread crumbs and baked in the oven, makes this pie something special. If you have trouble getting lobster meat, substitute shrimp.

4 tablespoons butter, plus 6 tablespoons melted

2 tablespoons flour

1½ cups lobster stock (see Source Guide)

¼ cup sherry

½ cup heavy cream

3 cups cooked Maine lobster meat cut into chunks

Salt and ground white pepper to taste

3 cups soft French bread crumbs

⅓ cup freshly grated Parmesan cheese

2 tablespoons chopped fresh flat-leaf parsley

In a 3-quart saucepan, melt the 4 tablespoons of butter and add the flour, whisking until it is smooth and bubbly. Gradually add the lobster stock, whisking until the bisque is smooth and thick, about 5 minutes. Add the sherry and cream, and bring the mixture to a boil. Reduce the heat to low and add the lobster meat. Taste the sauce, and adjust the seasoning with salt and white pepper. (At this point, the sauce may be refrigerated for 24 hours before assembling the pie.)

Preheat the oven to 375° F. Place the bread crumbs, cheese, and parsley in a large mixing bowl. Add the melted butter, and toss the mixture to coat the crumbs with the butter. Pour the lobster and sauce into a 9-inch round casserole that is 2½ inches deep. Top the casserole with the crumb mixture. Bake in the preheated oven for 20 minutes, or until the bread crumbs are toasted and golden brown.

Serves 6 to 8

Louisiana Crawfish Pie

*T*here are about as many recipes for crawfish pie as there are cooks in Louisiana, so I've taken my favorite parts from several recipes and incorporated them into this main dish pie. Generally, crawfish pies are hand-held or made in individual servings, but this one is wonderful to serve family-style. If you would like to make individual pies, cut the crust to fit your individual ramekins or baking dishes. If crawfish aren't available, substitute rock shrimp.

CRAWFISH FILLING
1 tablespoon vegetable oil
1 tablespoon butter
$^{1}/_{2}$ cup finely chopped onion
$^{1}/_{2}$ cup finely chopped green bell pepper
$^{1}/_{2}$ cup finely chopped celery
2 cloves garlic, minced
1 tablespoon Creole Seasoning (page 8)
2 tablespoons all-purpose flour
1$^{1}/_{2}$ pounds crawfish tails, peeled
2 teaspoons Worcestershire sauce
1$^{1}/_{2}$ teaspoons Tabasco sauce
$^{3}/_{4}$ cup heavy cream

1 recipe Louisiana Piecrust (see below)

In a 12-inch sauté pan, heat the vegetable oil and butter together. Add the onion, green pepper, celery, garlic, and Creole seasoning, and sauté for 3 to 4 minutes. Sprinkle the flour over the vegetables and cook, stirring, for 2 minutes. Add the crawfish, Worcestershire, Tabasco, and heavy cream, and bring the mixture to a boil. Simmer over medium heat for about 5 minutes, until the cream has reduced and the sauce is thickened.

Make the piecrust.

Preheat the oven to 375° F. Grease the edges of a 10-inch ovenproof baking dish, and transfer the crawfish mixture to the dish. Top the dish with the piecrust dough, and crimp the edges, making a few slits in the top of the crust to allow steam to escape. Bake the pie for 30 minutes, or until the crust is golden brown.

Louisiana Piecrust

1½ cups all-purpose flour
½ teaspoon Creole Seasoning (page 8)
¼ teaspoon salt
½ cup cold vegetable shortening
3 to 5 tablespoons ice water

Place the flour, Creole seasoning, and salt into the work bowl of a food processor and pulse on and off 3 times. Cut the cold shortening into small pieces and distribute it over the flour mixture. Pulse the machine on and off 3 times, until the shortening resembles peas. Sprinkle 3 tablespoons of ice water over the flour mixture, and pulse on and off until the dough begins to come together. If it appears dry, add more water, 1 teaspoon at a time. Turn the dough out onto a floured board, and roll into a disc approximately 12 inches in diameter. (The dough may be refrigerated for 8 hours, or frozen for up to 2 months.)

Serves 6 to 8

Seafood Brunch Pie Topped with Crab Cake Crust

*O*ne of my favorite brunch dishes is Eggs Benedict Louisiana Style, where the eggs and *English muffins are topped with crab cakes and hollandaise sauce. The theory of pot pies is to turn your favorite dishes into easy home cooking, and that is just what I have done here. You can make this as one huge pie, or you can make your guests individual pies. The crab cake for the crust can be made ahead and reheated when the pie bakes. The filling should be made at least a day before baking.*

1 recipe Crab Cake Crust (see below)

BRUNCH PIE
8 English muffins

6 eggs

1 1/4 cups heavy cream

1/4 cup flour

1/2 cup mayonnaise

1/4 cup chopped green onions

2 tablespoons freshly squeezed lemon juice

1 teaspoon salt

1/4 teaspoon cayenne

2 tablespoons melted butter

Prepare the crab cakes and refrigerate.

Spray an ovenproof baking dish, or individual ramekins, with non-stick cooking spray. Split the English muffins and place half of them in the bottom of the baking dish. (If you are using individual ramekins, use 1 muffin per person.)

In a large mixing bowl, whisk together the eggs, cream, flour, mayonnaise, green onions, lemon juice, salt, and cayenne. Pour the egg mixture over the English muffins and set the remaining muffins over the eggs. Cover the baking dish with plastic wrap and refrigerate it overnight.

When ready to serve, preheat the oven to 375° F. Remove the baking dish and cooked crab cakes from the refrigerator and allow them to sit at room temperature for 30 minutes. Top each English muffin with a crab cake. Brush the top with the melted butter, and bake for 30 to 40 minutes, until puffed and golden.

Crab Cake Crust

1 pound lump crab meat
$^1/_2$ cup fresh French bread crumbs
1 teaspoon Old Bay seasoning
$^1/_4$ cup mayonnaise
1 tablespoon Worcestershire sauce
2 tablespoons butter
1 tablespoon vegetable oil

In a mixing bowl, gently combine the crab meat, bread crumbs, Old Bay seasoning, mayonnaise, and Worcestershire. Form the mixture into 2-inch cakes. Cover and refrigerate for 2 hours. Heat the butter with the vegetable oil and sauté the crab cakes, about 3 minutes on each side, until golden brown. Drain on paper towels. Refrigerate the cooked crab cakes until ready to bake the brunch pie.

Serves 6 to 8

Seafood Pie with Shrimp Mashed Potato Crust

*C*overed *with a delicate pink crust concealing fresh fish and vegetables, this pie will delight your family and friends with its comforting flavors. Both filling and crust can be made ahead of time, then assembled and baked just before serving.*

1 recipe Shrimp Mashed Potato Crust (see below)

SEAFOOD FILLING
2 tablespoons butter
$^1/_2$ cup finely diced carrot
$^1/_2$ cup finely chopped onion
3 tablespoons flour
1$^1/_2$ cups chicken broth
$^1/_2$ cup milk
1 teaspoon salt
$^1/_4$ teaspoon freshly ground black pepper
1 cup fresh, or frozen and defrosted corn kernels
$^1/_4$ cup fresh, or frozen and defrosted petite green peas
2 pounds firm-fleshed fish fillets such as sea bass or halibut, cooked and cut into 1$^1/_2$-inch pieces

Prepare the crust and refrigerate.

In a 3-quart saucepan, melt the butter. Add the carrot and onion, and cook, stirring, until the vegetables are softened slightly, about 2–3 minutes. Add the flour, cooking and stirring until white bubbles form on the surface. Whisk in the broth and milk, stirring until thick and smooth. Season with the salt and pepper. Gently stir in the corn, peas, and fish. (Refrigerate at this point if you would like to prepare this filling ahead.)

When ready to serve, preheat the oven to 375° F. Transfer the filling to a 3-quart baking dish and spread the potato crust over the top of the pie. Bake

for 20 to 30 minutes, until the crust is golden and the pie is bubbling. Serve immediately.

Shrimp Mashed Potato Crust

Tiny bay shrimp sometimes don't have much flavor, sautéing them with butter, garlic, and Old Bay seasoning seems to help them along.

4 tablespoons butter

2 cloves garlic, mashed

$^1/_4$ pound tiny bay shrimp

1 tablespoon Old Bay seasoning

4 medium russet potatoes, boiled, drained, and mashed

$^1/_4$ cup heavy cream, or more as needed

2 egg yolks

In a small sauté pan, melt the butter. Add the garlic, and cook for 2 minutes, until the garlic begins to soften. Add the shrimp and sprinkle them with the Old Bay seasoning. Toss the shrimp in the butter, and set them aside.

Place the potatoes in a mixing bowl, and stir in the cream and egg yolks. Add the shrimp, and stir until blended. Taste for seasoning, and add additional cream if the potatoes seem stiff. Refrigerate.

Serves 6 to 8

Seafood Ragout Moët & Chandon

*M*y daughter's holiday office party featured this delectable pie as the main course, served with her company's client's champagne. She described the pot pie via e-mail and we made it together for New Year's Eve. With our apologies to the caterer, we think this version is easy and every bit as delicious as the one served at the party.

2 small bulbs fennel, cut into ¹/₂-inch slices

1¹/₂ cups baby carrots halved lengthwise

2 medium russet potatoes, cut into ¹/₂-inch dice

1 bay leaf

1 teaspoon salt, plus extra, to taste

¹/₂ teaspoon black peppercorns

3 cups water

5 tablespoons butter

4 tablespoons flour

¹/₂ teaspoon cayenne

1 cup reserved vegetable stock

1¹/₂ cups good champagne

³/₄ cup heavy cream

¹/₂ cup chopped fresh flat-leaf parsley

1 pound halibut fillets, cooked and cut into ¹/₂-inch chunks

1 pound large shrimp, peeled, deveined, and cooked

¹/₃ pound cooked crabmeat

1 (17¹/₂-ounce package) of frozen puff pastry, defrosted

1 European, hot house, or English cucumber (long, thin, wrapped in plastic)

2 medium carrots

2 teaspoons lemon juice

Preheat the oven to 400° F. In a 3-quart saucepan, combine the fennel, baby carrots, potatoes, bay leaf, 1 teaspoon salt, peppercorns, and water. Bring to a boil, and simmer for 5 to 7 minutes, until vegetables are just becoming tender. Remove the vegetables from the broth, and set them aside. Strain the broth and set it aside. In the same saucepan, melt 4 tablespoons of the butter and add the flour and cayenne, stirring with a whisk until the mixture is smooth and white bubbles begin to form. Gradually whisk in the vegetable stock and the champagne, stirring until the sauce is smooth and thick, about 4 to 6 minutes. Add the heavy cream and parsley, taste for seasoning, and add more salt and freshly ground black pepper.

Spray an ovenproof baking dish with non-stick cooking spray. Arrange the halibut, shrimp, and crab meat in the baking dish, spread the reserved vegetables over the top of the seafood, and cover with the sauce.

Roll out the puff pastry to fit the baking dish. Cover the dish with puff pastry, and crimp the edges with the tines of a fork. Slash 2 vent holes in the center and bake for 20 to 25 minutes, until the puff pastry is golden brown (see Note).

While the pie is cooking, cut the European cucumber and carrot into 2-inch matchsticks. In a small sauté pan, melt the remaining butter and sauté the vegetables for 2 minutes, until they soften. Add the lemon juice and toss to coat the vegetables. When the pie is done, garnish it with the cucumber and carrot mixture.

NOTE: If you would like to make individual pies, place equal amounts of seafood and vegetables in 8 individual ramekins, cover with the sauce and puff pastry cut to fit the baking dishes. Place the baking dishes on a cookie sheet and bake as directed, checking for doneness after 20 minutes.

Serves 6 to 8

Seafood Rockefeller Pot Pie

*O*ysters Rockefeller, a classic dish from the turn of the century, presented oysters on the half-shell covered with a creamed spinach mixture and baked on a bed of rock salt. For the pot pie version, we'll turn the pie upside down and use the spinach as the bottom crust, topping it with a delicate cream sauce filled with seafood. The pie can be assembled 2 days ahead and refrigerated until ready to bake.

SPINACH
2 tablespoons butter
2 (10-ounce) packages frozen chopped spinach, drained and squeezed dry
1 teaspoon salt
$^1/_2$ teaspoon freshly ground black pepper
Pinch of freshly grated nutmeg

SEAFOOD
1 pound mixed seafood of your choice (shrimp, scallops,
halibut, clams, crabmeat, or oysters)
$^1/_2$ cup white wine
2 tablespoons butter
2 tablespoons all-purpose flour
$^1/_4$ cup reserved poaching liquid
1$^1/_2$ cups milk
1 cup freshly grated Swiss cheese

Preheat the oven to 400° F.

In a sauté pan, heat the butter, add the spinach, and sauté just until wilted, 4 minutes. Season with salt, pepper, and nutmeg, and spread the spinach in an ovenproof baking dish.

Place the seafood in a sauté pan or poacher and add the white wine. Simmer until the seafood is cooked through, about 2–3 minutes. Set aside, draining and reserving the poaching liquid.

In a 3-quart saucepan, melt the butter, add the flour and cook until white bubbles begin to form. Whisk in the reserved poaching liquid and the milk, stirring until the sauce is thick and smooth. Stir in the cheese and set aside.

Cut the seafood into bite-sized chunks and spread it over the spinach. Top with the sauce, and bake in the preheated oven for 10 to 15 minutes, until the sauce is bubbling. Serve at once.

Serves 8

Shellfish Pie with Tarragon Artichoke Crust

*S*hrimp, crab, and scallops are quickly sautéed in butter and garlic, then topped with tarragon-scented artichoke hearts for an easy pie that is ready in under 30 minutes. For a dinner party, this dish is really nice if you prepare it in individual ramekins. Substitute fish fillets, such as sea bass or salmon, for a change.

3 tablespoons butter

2 cloves garlic, minced

2 pounds cleaned shellfish of your choice (shrimp, scallops,
crabmeat, oysters, clams, or mussels)

$^1/_4$ teaspoon cayenne

1 tablespoon olive oil

2 shallots, minced

2 (14$^1/_2$-ounce) cans artichoke hearts, drained and cut into quarters

$^1/_2$ cup heavy cream

1 tablespoon chopped fresh tarragon

$^1/_2$ teaspoon salt

$^1/_4$ teaspoon freshly ground black pepper

$^1/_3$ cup freshly grated Parmesan cheese

Preheat the broiler for 10 minutes. In a sauté pan, melt 2 tablespoons of the butter and add the garlic. Sauté for 1 to 2 minutes, until the garlic is softened. Add the shellfish, toss it in the garlic butter, and season with cayenne. Sauté the shellfish for 2 to 3 minutes. (The shellfish may not be cooked through, but it will finish cooking in the oven.) Remove from the heat and refrigerate the shellfish if you are not proceeding at once.

In another sauté pan, melt the remaining tablespoon of butter and the oil. Add the shallots and sauté for 2 minutes. Add the artichoke hearts and sauté for an additional 2 minutes, coating the artichokes with the butter mixture. Add the cream, salt, pepper, and tarragon, bringing the mixture to a boil.

Reduce the heat and simmer until the cream is reduced and thickened, about 4–5 minutes.

Spread the shellfish in an ovenproof baking dish that will hold it in one layer. Spread the artichoke heart crust over the shellfish, sprinkle with the Parmesan cheese and run the dish under the broiler until the cheese is melted and the fish is cooked, about 5 minutes. Serve immediately.

Serves 6 to 8

Cajun Shrimp Pie with Creamy Corn Crust

Spicy and creamy, this gorgeous pie is put together in 10 minutes, and is on the table in less than half an hour. The creamy topping is studded with red and green peppers and flavored with a bit of cayenne for a spicy kick. The shrimp steam gently under this beautiful crust.

1 1/2 pounds raw rock shrimp, peeled and deveined (if rock shrimp are unavailable, substitute medium shrimp, 36 to 40 per pound)

2 teaspoons Creole Seasoning (page 8)

2 tablespoons butter

1/4 cup finely chopped shallot

1/4 cup finely chopped green bell pepper

1/4 cup finely chopped red bell pepper

1/2 teaspoon cayenne

1/2 teaspoon salt

2 cups fresh, or frozen and defrosted white corn kernels

1/4 cup heavy cream (optional)

Preheat the oven to 375° F. Sprinkle the shrimp with the Creole seasoning, tossing until they are well coated. Place the shrimp in one layer in a 12-inch round ovenproof casserole or a deep pie plate.

In a sauté pan, melt the butter, add the shallots and peppers, and toss the mixture in the pan, adding the cayenne and salt. Sauté until the shallots become translucent, about 4 minutes.

Place the corn in a food processor or blender, and pulse on and off until the corn is creamy. Add the heavy cream, if using it, and process again. Pour the corn into the sauté pan with the shallot mixture and sauté for another 3 to 4 minutes. Spread the corn over the shrimp and bake for 15 minutes, until the corn is bubbling and the shrimp are pink.

Serves 6

Stuffed Shrimp Pie

*R*eminiscent of standard New England restaurant fare, this pie is both easy and elegant. Jumbo shrimp yield 21 to 25 per pound, 3 to 4 shrimp per person. If you can only find medium or large shrimp, buy 1 pound and follow the directions for the crust and baking.

4 tablespoons olive oil
20 jumbo shrimp, defrosted, peeled, deveined, and butterflied (see Note)
1 1/2 cups fresh French bread crumbs
1/2 teaspoon salt
1/4 teaspoon freshly ground black pepper
1/8 teaspoon cayenne
2 large cloves garlic, mashed
1/4 cup chopped fresh flat-leaf parsley
6 tablespoons melted butter
1/4 cup freshly grated Parmesan cheese
1/2 cup lump crab meat (if fresh crab is not available,
substitute 1/2 cup fresh bay shrimp)

Preheat the oven to 375° F. Pour 2 tablespoons of the oil into a 13 by 9-inch ovenproof baking dish. (You can use any flat baking dish that will hold the shrimp in one layer.) Lay the shrimp, cut side up, in the baking pan.

In a glass mixing bowl, stir together the bread crumbs, salt, pepper, cayenne, and garlic. Add the parsley, butter, cheese, and crabmeat to the bread crumbs, stirring until the mixture is well combined. Pour the crumb mixture over the shrimp in an even layer. Drizzle with the remaining olive oil. Bake in the preheated oven for 15 minutes, until the crumbs are golden and the shrimp are cooked through.

NOTE: To butterfly shrimp, split them down the back, leaving 1/4 to 1/2 inch intact. The shrimp will lay flat in the pan.

Serves 6

Mediterranean Shrimp Pie with Feta Crust

*F*or entertaining, this dish is a breeze, because it can be made up ahead of time and popped into a hot oven just before serving. I like to do this in individual ramekins with 4 jumbo shrimp for each person. If you would prefer to do this family-style, try using a paella pan, or a 13 by 9-inch ovenproof casserole dish. A side of minted orzo would be perfect.

4 tablespoons olive oil

2 pounds jumbo shrimp, peeled, deveined, and butterflied (see Note)

1 onion, finely chopped

1 bunch green onions, chopped (about $^1/_2$ cup)

3 cloves garlic, minced

1 tablespoon chopped fresh oregano or $1^1/_2$ teaspoons dried

2 teaspoons chopped fresh basil, or 1 teaspoon dried

3 cups peeled, seeded, and chopped fresh tomatoes,

or the equivalent canned, drained

1 teaspoon salt

$^3/_4$ teaspoon freshly ground black pepper

2 teaspoons sugar

$^1/_2$ cup white wine

$^1/_2$ pound feta cheese, crumbled

Chopped fresh flat-leaf parsley, for garnish

Oil the bottom of individual baking dishes with 2 tablespoons of the oil, and lay the shrimp flat in the bottom. Set the shrimp aside in the refrigerator while preparing the sauce. In a sauté pan, heat the remaining 2 tablespoons of oil. Add the onion, green onion, garlic, oregano, and basil, and sauté for 2 to 3 minutes. Add the tomatoes, salt, pepper, and sugar, and sauté for 5 to 8 minutes, until the tomatoes lose some of their juices. Add the wine, and allow it to boil off. Taste the sauce for salt and pepper, correcting the seasoning if necessary.

Simmer the sauce for 20 minutes. Remove it from the heat, and refrigerate until ready to serve (up to 3 days) or freeze for up to 1 month.

When you are ready to serve, preheat the oven to 375° F. Distribute the sauce among the baking dishes, and top each with crumbled feta. Bake the pie(s) for 15 minutes, until the cheese begins to melt and the shrimp are pink. Sprinkle the finished dish with the chopped fresh parsley.

NOTE: To butterfly shrimp, split them down the back, leaving ¼ to ½ inch intact. The shrimp will lay flat in the pan.

Serves 6 to 8

Down East Clam Pie with Bacon Biscuit Crust

*T*hick *New England–style clam chowder bakes underneath a savory bacon-flavored biscuit crust, making a hearty meal for a cold winter day. This easy pie can be made ahead of time and baked either in individual soup crocks or in a large ovenproof soup tureen and served family style.*

CLAM FILLING

4 tablespoons butter

1 cup finely chopped onion

3 tablespoons flour

2 cups water

1 cup clam juice

$1/2$ teaspoon salt, plus additional, to taste

6 shakes Tabasco sauce

$1/4$ teaspoon freshly ground black pepper, plus additional, to taste

3 cups red potatoes cut into $1/2$-inch dice

1 cup fresh, or frozen and defrosted corn kernels

2 dozen shucked hard-shelled clams, coarsely chopped (save the juice); or

2 (8-ounce) cans chopped clams (about 2 cups)

$1/2$ teaspoon dried thyme

2 cups light cream

1 recipe Bacon Biscuit Crust (see below)

2 tablespoons melted butter

In a 4-quart saucepan, melt the butter and stir in the chopped onion, cooking until the onion is translucent, and soft, about 3 minutes. Stir in the flour, and cook until the flour begins to bubble. Gradually whisk in the water, clam juice, $1/2$ teaspoon salt, Tabasco, and $1/4$ teaspoon pepper. Whisk until the mixture is smooth and bring to a boil. Add the potatoes and cook for 10 minutes. Add the corn and cook for an additional 10 minutes. Add the chopped clams and their juices, the thyme, and the cream, stirring until smooth. Reseason the mixture, and refrigerate it until you are ready to proceed.

Preheat the oven to 375° F. Make the crust. Place the crust on top of the pie, brush it with the melted butter, and bake for 20 to 25 minutes. Remove from the oven, and serve immediately.

Bacon Biscuit Crust

8 slices bacon, cooked, and crumbled
2¹/₂ cups all-purpose flour
1 tablespoon baking powder
1 teaspoon salt
1¹/₂ cups heavy cream

Place the bacon, flour, baking powder, and salt in a large mixing bowl. Stir in the cream, mixing with a fork until the dough begins to come together. Turn the dough out onto a floured board and knead it 3 or 4 times, until it becomes more firm. Roll the dough out ¹/₂ inch thick in the shape of your baking dish, or cut out individual biscuits.

Serves 6 to 8

Mussel Bisque Pie

A local restaurant serves this rich and creamy pie crowned with puff pastry. The waiter comes to the table with a bottle of Harvey's Bristol Cream sherry, plunges a soup spoon through the crust, and adds the sherry. I recommend serving individual pies to your guests. They make an awesome statement, and they're so easy to make up ahead of time.

1/2 cup butter

1 tablespoon tomato paste

1/4 cup all-purpose flour

4 cups lobster stock (see Source Guide)

2 tablespoons Cognac

1 cup heavy cream

Salt and freshly ground black pepper to taste

2 dozen green-lipped mussels, steamed and removed from their shells

1 (17 1/2-ounce) package frozen puff pastry, defrosted

1/2 cup Harvey's Bristol Cream sherry

In a heavy 4-quart saucepan over medium heat, melt the butter. Add the tomato paste, and whisk until blended. Add the flour and stir the mixture until the flour bubbles. Gradually add the lobster stock, whisking until the mixture is smooth, and the sauce comes to a boil, about 5 minutes. Turn the heat to low and add the Cognac, heavy cream, and mussels. Taste the sauce, and season it with salt and pepper. Keep the sauce warm over low heat.

Cut each piece of the defrosted puff pastry into 4 equal sections, and roll each piece so that it will fit over an individual soup bowl with about 1 inch overhang. Pour 2/3 cup of bisque into each soup bowl, placing 3 mussels in the bottom of each bowl. Cover the bisque with puff pastry, moistening the edges with water so they will adhere to the bowl. Refrigerate until ready to serve.

When ready to serve, preheat the oven to 400° F. Set the bowls at room temperature for 30 minutes, then bake for 20 to 25 minutes, until the pastry is puffed and golden.

When serving, poke a hole into the pastry and add 2 tablespoons of sherry to each serving.

Serves 6 to 8

Sherried Scallop Pie with Parmesan Puff Pastry Crust

A silken sherry bisque bursting with sea scallops and topped with a nutty Parmesan crust will make your guests so happy they came for dinner. I love to make individual pies, but feel free to make one large one. The sauce may be made ahead of time, and the pastry can be rolled out the day before and refrigerated until you are ready to use it.

4 tablespoons butter

4 tablespoons all-purpose flour

2 cups lobster stock (see Source Guide)

2 tablespoons sherry

$^{1}/_{4}$ cup heavy cream

$^{1}/_{4}$ teaspoon salt

$^{1}/_{8}$ teaspoon freshly ground black pepper

Pinch of grated nutmeg

$1^{1}/_{2}$ pounds sea scallops, cut in half

$^{3}/_{4}$ cup freshly grated Parmesan cheese

1 ($17^{1}/_{2}$-ounce) package frozen puff pastry, defrosted

In a 4-quart saucepan, melt the butter and add the flour. Cook over medium-high heat, whisking until the flour is smooth. Add the lobster stock and whisk until the sauce comes to a boil. Add the sherry and heavy cream, and season with the salt and freshly ground pepper. Add the nutmeg and remove the sauce from the heat. Add the scallops to the sauce, and refrigerate until ready to finish the pie.

Preheat the oven to 400° F. Place $^{3}/_{4}$ cup of sauce and scallops into each of 6 individual baking dishes. Sprinkle some of the Parmesan cheese on a board and roll out both sheets of puff pastry, using the Parmesan as you would flour. Cut the puff pastry 1 inch larger than your baking dishes. Cover the filling with the puff pastry, crimping the edges with the tines of a fork. Make a slit in the top of the pastry to allow the steam to escape. Bake the pies for 20 minutes, until the pastry is golden brown.

Serves 6

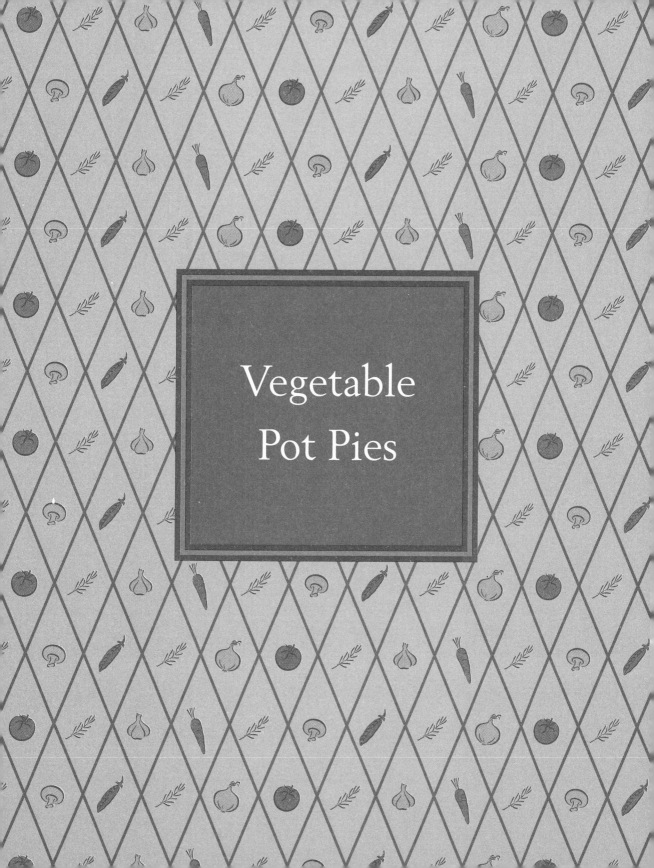

Vegetable
Pot Pies

Artichoke and Mushroom Pie

Asparagus and Leek Pie

Broccoli Hollandaise Pie

Chili Relleno Pie

Corn, Zucchini, and Tomato Pie

Goat Cheese and Tomato Pie

Grilled Vegetable Pie with Ricotta Spinach Crust

Mediterranean Eggplant Pie

Minestrone Pie with Parmesan Focaccia Crust

Mom's Macaroni and Cheese with Parmesan Crumb Crust

Pie à la Milanaise

Pizza Pie Potatoes

Portobello Mushroom Pie

Potato Florentine Pie

Roasted Tomato Pie with Spinach Pesto Crust

Southwestern Vegetable Pie with Tortilla Crust

Spinach, Artichoke, and Feta Pie

Swiss Chard Pie with Bruschetta Crust

Wild Rice Pie with Blue Cheese Onion Crust

Zucchini Pie with Parmesan Rice Crust

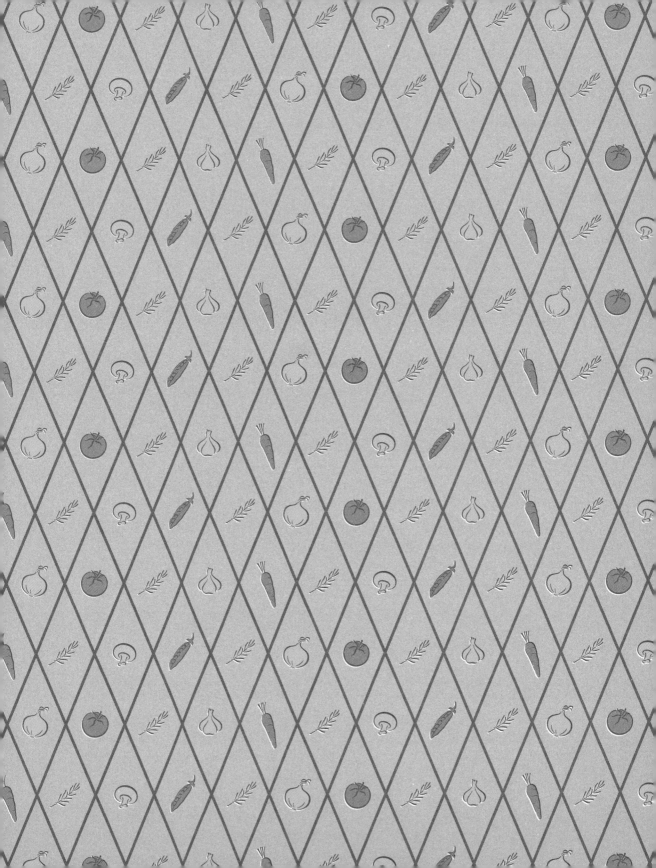

M OM'S exhortation to "eat your vegetables" was made because she wanted you to grow up big and strong, or maybe it was to get rid of that gray plate of limp broccoli. That childhood image of overcooked vegetables haunts many people today, and they have completely sworn off anything green. My daughter and I took her new roommate out for a pizza, and asked if there was anything she didn't want on it. "Oh whatever you want is fine," she replied. We ordered the deep dish vegetarian from Gino's in Chicago, and this young lady proceeded to peel off each and every vegetable on the pie, until all that was left (if you could call it that) was cheese and crust, and a pathetic pile of peppers, onions, mushrooms, and artichoke hearts. I was heartbroken to think that this girl would never experience the joy of biting into a crisp green bean glistening with olive oil and lemon juice, or the simple pleasure of eating a piece of steamed asparagus.

This chapter is dedicated to all those who love their veggies, and mostly to those who think they don't. Sometimes disguising things helps to make them look different so we're able to try them. With this in mind, I think the vegetable pot pie is a concept whose time has come. We'll enclose Portobello mushrooms covered with a simple tomato sauce and slivers of Parmigiano-Reggiano in flaky phyllo for a wonderful light dinner.

We'll make a Southwestern pie from green chilies, eggs, corn, and Monterey Jack cheese, and cover it with corn tortillas. Also, we'll grill vegetables and top them with a spinach and ricotta crust that will make your meat and potatoes man beg for more.

Most of us have an endless variety of fresh vegetables available year round. For others, the climate dictates the seasonality and variety of fresh vegetables. For some dishes in this chapter, frozen and some canned varieties are acceptable alternatives to fresh. But for some vegetables, there is no acceptable alternative, and I would wait to try those until they are in season. Specifically, vine-ripened tomatoes are something that cannot be duplicated. If you absolutely cannot live without the goat cheese and tomato tart in the dead of winter, I suggest spending the extra money and finding a greengrocer that carries vine-ripened tomatoes. I guarantee that the next time you serve a veggie pot pie, your family will clean their plates.

Artichoke and Mushroom Pie

*T*his delectable pie comes from a dish served in the Kennedy White House. It was served as a side dish back then and featured in Life magazine. I have made it into a fabulous main course, covered with puff pastry rolled in Parmesan cheese. This is one instance where a bottom crust really sets off the pie.

$^1/_2$ cup freshly grated Parmesan cheese

1 (17$^1/_2$-ounce) package frozen puff pastry sheets, defrosted

2 tablespoons butter

1 pound white mushrooms, cleaned and sliced $^1/_2$ inch thick

2 tablespoons freshly squeezed lemon juice

1$^1/_2$ teaspoons salt

$^1/_2$ teaspoon freshly ground black pepper

2 tablespoons flour

1 cup heavy cream

2 (14-ounce) cans artichoke hearts, drained and cut in half

$^1/_2$ cup freshly grated Swiss cheese

Preheat the oven to 400° F. Sprinkle half the Parmesan cheese on a board, and roll 1 sheet of puff pastry into a 12 by 10-inch rectangle, using the cheese as you would flour. Place the sheet of puff pastry on a 15 by 10-inch jelly-roll pan that has been lined with parchment or aluminum foil. Roll out the other piece of pastry in the same manner. Refrigerate both pieces of pastry while you are making the filling.

In a sauté pan, melt the butter, add the mushrooms, and cook until the liquid in the pan begins to evaporate, about 4–6 minutes. Sprinkle the lemon juice over the mushrooms, and season them with salt and pepper. Sprinkle the flour over the mushrooms, and stir until the flour begins to cook. Gradually add the

recipe continues on following page

continued from previous page

cream, about 3 minutes, whisking until the mixture is smooth and thick. Add the artichoke hearts. (The filling can be refrigerated at this point if you're making it ahead of time.)

Spread the filling over the chilled bottom crust and top with Swiss cheese. Cover with the top crust, and slash a few vent holes in the top. Crimp the edges with a fork or decorative tool and bake the pie for 20 to 25 minutes, until the pastry is golden and puffed.

Serves 6 to 8

Asparagus and Leek Pie

*E*legant asparagus, and creamy leeks combine under a crispy phyllo crust for a sensational entrée pie. It can be made up to 24 hours ahead of time and refrigerated until baking.

$^1/_2$ cup melted butter, plus 2 tablespoons cold butter

3 quarts water

1 pound asparagus, trimmed and cut into 1-inch pieces

2 medium-sized leeks, washed and thinly sliced, using the white and only a bit of the tender green part

1 teaspoon salt

$^1/_2$ teaspoon freshly ground black pepper

2 cups freshly grated imported Swiss cheese

$^1/_4$ cup chopped fresh dill weed

1 cup dry bread crumbs

$^1/_2$ cup freshly grated Parmesan cheese

2 tablespoons chopped fresh flat-leaf parsley

$^1/_2$ pound frozen phyllo dough, thawed

Preheat the oven to 375° F. Brush a 13 by 9-inch ovenproof pan with some of the melted butter.

In a pot, bring the water to a boil, add the asparagus, and remove them after 1 minute. Drain the asparagus, pat them dry, and place them in a mixing bowl.

In a sauté pan, heat the 2 tablespoons of butter, add the leeks, and sauté until they are limp, about 4–6 minutes. Add the leeks to the asparagus, along with the salt, pepper, Swiss cheese, and dill. Gently stir to combine.

Place the bread crumbs, Parmesan, and parsley in a bowl and stir to blend. Lay the phyllo on a clean counter and cover it with a clean kitchen towel. Lay 1 sheet of phyllo in the bottom of the prepared pan and brush it all over with

recipe continues on following page

continued from previous page

melted butter, then sprinkle it with some of the crumbs. Continue to layer the phyllo sheets this way until you have 5 layers. Pour the asparagus mixture into the baking dish. Place another sheet of phyllo on top of the asparagus, brush it with butter, sprinkle it with crumbs, and continue to layer the sheets until there are 4 more layers of phyllo. Brush the last sheet with butter and sprinkle it with crumbs. Tuck the ends of the phyllo in around the baking dish. (At this point the pie may be covered with plastic wrap and refrigerated for up to 24 hours.)

When you are ready to bake the pie, remove it from the refrigerator and allow it to sit at room temperature for 30 minutes. Remove the plastic wrap and bake the pie in the preheated oven for 35 to 45 minutes, until the phyllo is golden brown. Allow the pie to rest for 5 minutes before cutting it.

VARIATION: This pie is so versatile, we have used strips of prosciutto or shrimp in it for a non-vegetarian meal.

Serves 6 to 8

Broccoli Hollandaise Pie

Broccoli is a vegetable people either love or hate, as evidenced by its banishment from the White House some years ago. I'm convinced that if the President had been served this pie, he wouldn't have been able to resist the bottom rice crust filled with steamed broccoli and crowned with a light-as-a-feather hollandaise topping.

RICE AND BROCCOLI FILLING

2 cups cooked rice

1 egg, beaten

2 tablespoons melted butter

$^1/_2$ teaspoon salt

3 shakes Tabasco sauce

4 cups steamed broccoli florets, tossed with salt and pepper to taste

1 recipe Hollandaise Crust (see below)

In a large bowl, stir together the rice, egg, melted butter, salt, and Tabasco. Spray a 10-inch ovenproof dish with non-stick cooking spray. Press the rice mixture into the bottom of the pan. Arrange the broccoli over the rice.

Preheat the oven to 400° F. Make the crust. Spread the sauce/crust over the broccoli. Bake in the oven for 25 minutes, until the crust is golden and set. Let the pie stand for 5 minutes before cutting it into wedges and serving.

recipe continues on following page

continued from previous page

Hollandaise Crust

*This is a take-off on sauce mousseline, in which stiffly whipped
cream was folded into a hollandaise. Make this just before baking, so that
the crust will puff up nicely.*

3 egg yolks
2 tablespoons freshly squeezed lemon juice, plus additional to taste
2 tablespoons finely chopped fresh flat-leaf parsley
1 tablespoon finely chopped fresh chives
$^1/_2$ teaspoon dry mustard
$^1/_2$ teaspoon salt, plus additional to taste
3 shakes Tabasco sauce
$^3/_4$ cup hot melted butter
$^1/_2$ cup heavy cream, stiffly whipped

Place the egg yolks, 2 tablespoons of lemon juice, the parsley, chives, mustard, $^1/_2$ teaspoon of salt, and Tabasco into the work bowl of a food processor or blender. Blend for 1 minute. With the motor running, gradually add the hot butter through the feed tube until the sauce thickens, about 30 seconds. Taste for seasoning, and add more salt or lemon juice as needed. Remove from the work bowl, and turn into a mixing bowl. Fold in the whipping cream.

Serves 6 to 8

Chile Relleno Pie

A	*new twist on an old stand-by, this easy vegetarian pie features roasted chile peppers stuffed with Monterey Jack cheese and baked under a cornmeal soufflé flavored with corn and Colby cheese. Stuff the chilies and make the sauce the night before, then combine the other ingredients just before baking.*

1 recipe Fresh Tomato Salsa (see below)

2 (7-ounce) cans whole green roasted chile peppers (see Note)

1 pound Monterey Jack cheese, cut into $1/2$-inch logs

3 tablespoons butter

$1/2$ cup finely chopped onion

$1/4$ cup finely chopped red bell pepper

3 tablespoons yellow cornmeal

1 tablespoon all-purpose flour

1 cup milk

1 teaspoon salt

$1/8$ teaspoon cayenne

1 cup fresh, or frozen and defrosted corn kernels

5 egg yolks

7 egg whites, stiffly beaten

1 cup freshly grated Colby cheese

Make the salsa ahead of time and refrigerate.

Preheat the oven to 350° F. Grease a 13 by 9-inch ovenproof casserole dish. Drain and rinse the chilies. Stuff each chile with Monterey Jack cheese. Lay the chilies in the casserole dish in 1 layer.

In a 2-quart saucepan, melt the butter. Add the onion and red pepper, and cook for 2 to 3 minutes, until the vegetables begin to soften. Sprinkle with the

recipe continues on following page

continued from previous page

cornmeal and flour, and cook, stirring, until the flour begins to bubble, about 2–3 minutes. Gradually add the milk, whisking until the sauce is smooth and thick, about 4–5 minutes. Add the salt and cayenne, and transfer the sauce to a bowl. Beat in the corn and egg yolks. Cover and refrigerate the sauce until you are ready to proceed. When ready to bake pie, fold the egg whites into the sauce. Spread the crust over the chilies in the baking dish and sprinkle the top with the grated cheese. Bake for 25 minutes, until the crust is set and the cheese is golden. Serve with the fresh tomato salsa.

Fresh Tomato Salsa

4 cups chopped fresh tomatoes

$^1/_2$ cup tomato puree

$^1/_3$ cup finely chopped onion

1 clove garlic, minced

2 jalapeño chile peppers, seeded and chopped

2 tablespoons chopped fresh cilantro

1 tablespoon chopped fresh oregano

1 teaspoon salt

$^1/_2$ teaspoon freshly ground black pepper

2 tablespoons lime juice

In a glass bowl, combine all the ingredients and toss together. Refrigerate the salsa for at least 4 hours before serving.

NOTE: If you would prefer to roast your own peppers, use 8 Anaheim chile peppers, and broil until the skins are charred. Turn off the heat, and leave the peppers in the oven for 30 minutes. (The steam in the oven will loosen the skins.) Peel the skins off the peppers, and slit them to remove the seeds and stuff with the cheese.

Serves 6 to 8

Corn, Zucchini, and Tomato Pie

*T*his pie is made from the overflowing bounty of the backyard garden. Fresh corn and zucchini seasoned with dill bake underneath Parmesan-crusted tomatoes to make a scrumptious entrée that can be served warm or at room temperature.

3 cups fresh, or frozen and defrosted corn kernels

5 small zucchini, cut into matchstick pieces

2 teaspoons salt

1 teaspoon freshly ground black pepper

1 tablespoon fresh dill weed

2 tablespoons melted butter

3 to 4 vine-ripened tomatoes, cut into $1/2$-inch slices

$1/2$ cup freshly grated Parmesan cheese

$1/4$ cup dry bread crumbs

2 tablespoons olive oil

Preheat the oven to 375° F. In a 13 by 9-inch ovenproof baking dish, combine the corn, zucchini, 1 teaspoon of salt, $1/2$ teaspoon of pepper, the dill, and the melted butter, tossing to coat the vegetables. Cover the vegetables with the tomatoes. Sprinkle with the remaining salt and pepper.

In a small bowl, combine the cheese and bread crumbs. Sprinkle the mixture over the tomatoes and drizzle with the olive oil. Bake the pie for 30 minutes, or until the cheese is bubbling. Remove it from the oven, and let it stand for 5 minutes before serving.

Serves 6 to 8

Goat Cheese and Tomato Pie

*T*his pie is similar to a pizza, with the tomatoes forming the top crust and the rosemary focaccia as the bottom crust. It's delicious served warm, but is also nice at room temperature.

FOCACCIA
2¹/₂ tablespoons active dry yeast

1 cup warm water (105° F.)

1 teaspoon sugar

3¹/₄ cups all-purpose flour or bread flour

1 teaspoon salt

1 tablespoon extra virgin olive oil

1¹/₄ teaspoons crumbled dried rosemary

GOAT CHEESE FILLING
¹/₂ cup chopped fresh spinach

8 ounces mild soft goat cheese

4 tablespoons butter

1 egg

¹/₂ teaspoon freshly ground black pepper

1 recipe Tomato Crust (see below)

To make the focaccia, combine the yeast, water, and sugar in a 2-cup measure. Stir the yeast, and let it stand for 5 minutes, until the yeast bubbles. Place the flour and salt in a food processor or mixing bowl, add the yeast mixture, the olive oil, and the rosemary, and blend. If you are mixing by hand, turn the dough out onto a floured board and knead it 10 times. If you are using the food processor, process until the dough forms a ball. Place the dough in an oiled bowl and let it rise in a warm draft-free place for 45 minutes, until it has doubled in bulk. Punch down the dough and roll it out to fit a 10 by 15-inch jellyroll pan. Refrigerate until ready to bake.

In a mixing bowl, blend the spinach into the goat cheese, butter, and egg. Season the mixture with black pepper and refrigerate it until ready to bake.

When ready to bake the pie, preheat the oven to 375° F. Make the crust. Spread the filling over the focaccia.

Distribute the tomato crust evenly over the top of the pie. Bake the pie for 25 minutes, until the cheese is set. Cool for 10 minutes before serving.

Tomato Crust

6 vine-ripened plum or Roma tomatoes, sliced ¼ inch thick

2 cloves garlic, minced

¼ cup extra virgin olive oil

¼ cup chopped fresh basil

1 teaspoon salt

½ teaspoon freshly ground black pepper

2 tablespoons freshly grated lemon zest

Arrange the tomato slices over the goat cheese filling. In a bowl, combine the garlic, olive oil, basil, salt, pepper, and lemon zest.

Serves 6 to 8

Grilled Vegetable Pie with Ricotta Spinach Crust

*G*rilled vegetables bake under a cloudlike ricotta and spinach crust, creating a delectable pie for lunch, brunch, or dinner. Feel free to substitute your favorite vegetables,
a layer of cooked pasta, or tofu.

1 cup olive oil

1^1/$_2$ teaspoons salt

^{1}/$_2$ teaspoon freshly ground black pepper

3 cloves garlic, crushed

2 (6-inch) zucchini, sliced lengthwise into ^{1}/$_2$-inch slices

2 yellow squash, sliced lengthwise into ^{1}/$_2$-inch slices

3 Portobello mushrooms

1 large red onion, sliced ^{1}/$_2$ inch thick

1 eggplant (about ^{3}/$_4$ to 1 pound), peeled and sliced into ^{1}/$_2$-inch-thick rounds

2 large tomatoes, sliced into ^{1}/$_2$-inch-thick rounds

1 recipe Ricotta Spinach Crust (see below)

Preheat the broiler for 10 minutes, or preheat a gas or charcoal grill. In a glass
measuring cup, combine the oil with the salt, pepper, and garlic. Line 2 baking
sheets with aluminum foil. Place the vegetables on the baking sheets, brushing
them with some of the seasoned oil. Broil until the vegetables are tender, turning them once and brushing them again with the oil. Remove the vegetables
from the trays and slice the mushrooms into ^{1}/$_2$-inch-thick slices. Prepare the
Ricotta spinach crust.

Preheat the oven to 375 degrees. Grease a 13 by 9-inch pan, and layer the
vegetables in the pan. Spread the crust over the vegetables, smoothing the top.
(The pie can be refrigerated for 24 hours before baking.) When ready to bake,
sprinkle the additional Parmesan cheese over the top. Bake for 35 to 40 minutes, until the topping is puffed and golden.

Ricotta Spinach Crust

2 cups ricotta cheese

2 eggs

$^3/_4$ cup freshly grated Parmesan cheese

1 cup fresh spinach, finely chopped

$^1/_4$ teaspoon grated nutmeg

In a mixing bowl, combine the ricotta, eggs, $^1/_2$ cup of the Parmesan, the spinach, and the nutmeg. Refrigerate the crust until ready to use.

Serves 8

Mediterranean Eggplant Pie

*A*spicy eggplant mixture tops this pie, which is a cross between a traditional pastitsio—a Greek lasagne-type dish—and a meatless moussaka. Japanese eggplant are generally more tender, but if they are not available, substitute purple eggplant. The entire pie can be made ahead of time and refrigerated for up to 2 days, or frozen for 1 month.

EGGPLANT AND PASTA
1 tablespoon olive oil
1 large onion, chopped
$1/2$ cup finely chopped carrot
$1/2$ cup finely chopped celery
4 cloves garlic, minced
5 cups $1/2$-inch Japanese eggplant, diced cubes
1 teaspoon salt, plus additional to taste
$1/2$ teaspoon freshly ground black pepper, plus additional to taste
2 teaspoons chopped fresh oregano or 1 teaspoon dried
2 teaspoons chopped fresh basil, or 1 teaspoon dried
$1/4$ cup dry red wine
1 cup beef broth (if you decide to keep this vegetarian, use vegetable broth or water)
1 cup tomato purée
$1/4$ cup chopped fresh flat-leaf parsley

1 recipe Cream Sauce (see below)
1 pound small pasta, such as elbow macaroni, cooked and drained
4 ounces feta cheese, crumbled

In a 12-inch sauté pan, heat the oil. Add the onion, carrot, and celery, and sauté, until the onion is translucent, about 3 minutes. Add the garlic and sauté for another minute. Stir in the eggplant, 1 teaspoon of salt, $1/2$ teaspoon of pepper, the oregano, and basil, and cook until the eggplant becomes soft, about 4–6 minutes. Add the wine and broth, stirring the vegetables. Mix in the tomato puree and simmer for 10 minutes, until the liquid is almost absorbed. Season the mixture with more salt and pepper, and stir in the parsley. Set the mixture aside while you make the cream sauce. (At this point, the eggplant may be refrigerated for 2 days before assembling the final dish.)

Preheat the oven to 350° F. Butter a 3-quart casserole or 13 by 9-inch pan. Spread a layer of cream sauce in the bottom of the pan, and top it with half of the pasta. Spoon some of the cream sauce over the pasta, and top it with half of the eggplant mixture. Spread the remaining pasta over the eggplant, spooning the remaining cream sauce over the top. Cover the sauce with the remaining eggplant and top it with the feta. Tent the casserole with foil and bake it for 30 minutes. Remove the foil and bake for another 15 minutes. Let the casserole rest for 5 minutes before cutting it.

Cream Sauce

4 tablespoons butter

6 tablespoons flour

3½ cups milk

⅓ cup freshly grated Parmesan cheese

1 teaspoon salt

¼ teaspoon ground white pepper

⅛ teaspoon freshly grated nutmeg

In a 3-quart saucepan over medium-high heat, melt the butter. Add the flour, and cook the roux until white bubbles begin to form. Slowly whisk in the milk, stirring until the sauce comes to a boil, about 5 minutes. Remove the sauce from the heat. Stir in the cheese, salt, pepper, and nutmeg.

Serves 6 to 8

Minestrone Pie with Parmesan Focaccia Crust

C old winter days deserve comfort food, like this hearty vegetable stew. The soup can be prepared ahead of time, and the focaccia can be made and stored in a Ziploc bag in the refrigerator until you are ready to cover the pie.

MINESTRONE
2 tablespoons extra virgin olive oil

1 cup chopped onion

2 cups coarsely chopped carrots

4 stalks celery, coarsely chopped

2 cups chopped tomatoes

$1/2$ cup white wine

4 cups vegetable broth

$1^{1}/_{2}$ teaspoons salt, plus additional to taste

$1/2$ teaspoon freshly ground black pepper, plus additional to taste

2 teaspoons fresh crumbled rosemary, or 1 teaspoon dried

2 small zucchini, sliced into $1/2$-inch rounds

1 cup green beans cut into 1-inch lengths

2 medium russet potatoes, cut into $1/2$-inch cubes

3 cups coarsely chopped spinach, Swiss chard, or escarole

2 cups canned small white beans, drained and rinsed

Rind of Parmigiano-Reggiano cheese, 2-inch square (optional)

1 recipe Parmesan Focaccia (see below)

1 tablespoon extra virgin olive oil

2 tablespoons freshly grated Parmesan

$1^{1}/_{2}$ teaspoons fresh crumbled rosemary, $1/2$ teaspoon dried

In a stockpot, heat the oil and add the onion, carrots, and celery. Sauté until the vegetables are soft, about 3 minutes. Add the tomatoes and white wine, and cook for three minutes. Add the vegetable broth, $1^{1}/_{2}$ teaspoons of salt, $1/2$ teaspoon of pepper, the rosemary, zucchini, green beans, potatoes, spinach, and white beans. Simmer uncovered for 10 minutes. Add the Parmigiano-Reggiano rind, if using it, and simmer another 40 minutes. Taste for seasoning before covering the soup. (The soup may be refrigerated for 3 days or frozen for up to 2 months.)

Make the focaccia crust.

Preheat the oven to 350° F. When you are ready to bake the minestrone pie, pour the soup into an ovenproof baking dish and roll out the dough to fit the dish. If you would like to make individual servings, fill 8 ramekins with soup, leaving 1 inch at the top for the focaccia to expand. Float the focaccia on top of the stew, brush it with the olive oil, and sprinkle it with the Parmesan and the rosemary. Bake for 35 to 45 minutes, until the top is golden brown.

Parmesan Focaccia

1¼ cups warm water (105° to 110° F.)

2 teaspoons active dry yeast

1 teaspoon sugar

1 teaspoon salt

3 cups flour

½ cup freshly grated Parmesan cheese

2 tablespoons extra virgin olive oil

Place the water in a 2-cup measure. Stir in the yeast and sugar. Set the mixture aside for 10 minutes, or until it bubbles. Place the salt, flour, and Parmesan in a mixing bowl or the work bowl of a food processor. Blend the yeast into the flour and gradually add the olive oil. Turn the dough out onto a floured board and knead it 4 times. Place the dough into an oiled bowl covered with a clean kitchen towel and set it aside to rise for 45 minutes to 1 hour. The focaccia can be stored in an oiled Ziploc bag in the refrigerator until you are ready to roll it out and fit it over the baking dish.

NOTE: The cheese rind becomes soft and flavors the soup as it cooks.

Serves 8

Mom's Macaroni and Cheese with Parmesan Crumb Crust

*W*e *all grew up with that blue box of macaroni and the Day-Glo cheese, but now we are ready for something better. This macaroni and cheese has a smooth but sharp Cheddar cheese sauce, and it's covered with an ethereal Parmesan crumb crust. I use elbow macaroni to be traditional, but you could use small shell pasta, or your favorite shape.*

MACARONI AND CHEESE
6 quarts water

1 pound elbow macaroni

4 tablespoons butter

1 clove garlic, minced

3 tablespoons all-purpose flour

$1/4$ teaspoon Tabasco sauce, plus additional to taste

3 cups milk

$1/2$ cup heavy cream

4 cups freshly grated sharp Cheddar cheese

1 teaspoon salt, plus additional to taste

$1/2$ teaspoon freshly ground black pepper, plus additional to taste

$1/2$ teaspoon dry mustard

1 recipe Parmesan Crumb Crust (see below)

Grease a 13 by 9-inch ovenproof casserole. In a large pot, bring the water to a boil and cook the macaroni al dente, according to the package directions. Drain the macaroni and stir in 1 tablespoon of the butter. Set it aside.

In a 4-quart saucepan, melt the remaining 3 tablespoons of butter. Add the garlic and sauté for 1 minute. Add the flour, and whisk until it begins to bubble. Add the $1/4$ teaspoon of Tabasco and gradually whisk in the milk, bringing the sauce to a boil. Reduce the heat to low and gradually add the cream, Cheddar cheese, 1 teaspoon of salt, $^1/_2$ teaspoon of pepper, and the mustard, whisking until the cheese has melted and the sauce is smooth. Taste the sauce for seasoning and add additional salt, pepper, or Tabasco. Stir the sauce into the macaroni, and transfer the mixture to the prepared baking dish. (At this point the macaroni may be refrigerated for up to 2 days. Allow the casserole to sit at room temperature for 30 minutes before baking.)

Make the crust. Preheat the oven to 375° F. Spread the bread crumbs evenly over the casserole and bake it in the preheated oven for 30 minutes, or until the pie is bubbling and the crumbs are golden.

Parmesan Crumb Crust

4 tablespoons butter
2$^1/_2$ cups dry bread crumbs
$^3/_4$ cup freshly grated Parmesan cheese
2 tablespoons chopped fresh flat-leaf parsley

In a sauté pan, melt the butter. Add the bread crumbs, and toss until they are well coated. Add the cheese and parsley, stirring to combine. Transfer the crumbs to a bowl and refrigerate until ready to use.

Serves 6 to 8

Pie à la Milanaise

*M*y favorite French bakery serves this pie as a luncheon dish, so I had to eat a lot of these to come up with just the right recipe. I think the chef thought I was flirting with him when I became a regular at lunch! You'll understand what motivated me after you've tasted this delectable pie, layered with mushrooms, roasted red peppers, cheese, spinach, and eggs, all wrapped up in golden puff pastry.

5 tablespoons butter

¾ pound white mushrooms, sliced ½ inch thick

1 sheet frozen puff pastry, rolled out ¼ inch thick (about 12 by 10 inches)

3 red bell peppers, roasted (see Note)

2 cups freshly grated Swiss cheese

2 shallots, minced

6 cups fresh spinach, stems cut

1 teaspoon salt

¾ teaspoon freshly ground black pepper

¼ teaspoon grated nutmeg

3 eggs, beaten with 1 tablespoon water

Preheat the oven to 400° F. Place the puff pastry on a cookie sheet lined with parchment or foil. In a sauté pan, melt 2 tablespoons of the butter. Add the mushrooms, salt, and pepper, and sauté until they begin to soften, about 3–4 minutes. Remove the mushrooms from the pan with a slotted spoon, draining off any liquid that may have accumulated. Spread them onto the center of the puff pastry in an 8-inch circle. Cut the red peppers into strips and lay them over the mushrooms. Cover the peppers with ½ cup of the Swiss cheese. In the same sauté pan, melt an additional 2 tablespoons and sauté the shallots for 2 minutes. Add the spinach and season it with the salt, pepper, and nutmeg. Cook the spinach until it begins to wilt. Spread the spinach over the pie and top it with $^1\!/_2$ cup of the remaining cheese. Whisk together the egg-water mixture. Heat another tablespoon of butter in the sauté pan, and cook the eggs as you would an omelette, until set but not dry. Top the pie with the omelette, and cover it with the remaining cheese. Bring the 4 corners of the puff pastry together at the center, and twist them into a knot. (Refrigerate the pie for up to 8 hours—optional.) Bake the pie for 20 to 30 minutes, until the pastry is golden. This pie is great hot, but it is also delicious at room temperature.

NOTE: To roast red peppers, preheat the broiler and broil the peppers until the skin is charred all over. Turn off the heat and leave the peppers in the oven for 30 minutes. The steam in the oven will make it easier to remove the skins. Remove the skins from the peppers and proceed as directed.

Serves 6 to 8

Pizza Pie Potatoes

*S*picy pizza flavors and thinly sliced potatoes combine for a vegetarian dinner that will make your family members of the Clean Plate Club. The tomato sauce may be made ahead and stored in the refrigerator or freezer.

TOMATO SAUCE

¹/₄ cup olive oil

2 cloves garlic, minced

1 cup chopped onion

6 cups chopped canned plum tomatoes

2 tablespoons chopped fresh basil, or 1¹/₂ teaspoons dried

2 tablespoons chopped fresh flat-leaf parsley

1 tablespoon chopped fresh oregano, or 1¹/₂ teaspoons dried

1 teaspoon salt, plus additional to taste

¹/₂ teaspoon freshly ground black pepper, plus additional to taste

1 tablespoon sugar

POTATO PIE

4 medium russet potatoes, cut ¹/₄ inch thick

2 teaspoons salt

1 teaspoon freshly ground black pepper

1¹/₂ cups vegetable broth

2 cups freshly grated mozzarella cheese

¹/₂ cup freshly grated Parmesan cheese

1 tablespoon chopped fresh oregano, or 1¹/₂ teaspoon dried

2 tablespoons extra virgin olive oil

To make the sauce, in a 3-quart saucepan, heat the oil and add the garlic and onion. Sauté until the vegetables are softened, about 2–3 minutes. Add the tomatoes, herbs, and seasonings, and cook uncovered for 30 minutes. Taste the sauce and correct the seasoning. (The sauce may be refrigerated for up to 2 days, or frozen for up to 2 months.)

When ready to make the potatoes, preheat the oven to 400° F. Spray a 13 by 9-inch baking dish or other ovenproof dish with non-stick cooking spray. Spread a third of the potatoes in the bottom of the pan. Sprinkle with some of the salt and pepper. Spread a third of the tomato sauce over the potatoes. Repeat the layering twice more, ending with a layer of tomato sauce. Pour the vegetable broth over the casserole. Cover with the grated cheeses, and sprinkle with the oregano. Drizzle the oil over the top of the pie. Cover the pie with foil, and bake for 35 minutes. Uncover and bake for an additional 30 minutes, until the potatoes are tender.

Serves 6 to 8

Portobello Mushroom Pie

*E*ncased in flaky phyllo, meaty Portobello mushrooms pair with a spicy tomato sauce, and Parmigiano-Reggiano cheese to produce a mouth-watering pie for a light supper. Serve it with a tossed green salad, and you will never call for a pizza delivery again!

1 teaspoon butter

3 Portobello mushrooms (about 6 ounces), sliced $1/2$ inch thick

1 tablespoon olive oil

$1/2$ cup chopped onion

1 ($14^{1}/2$-ounce) can chopped tomatoes with their juice

1 teaspoon salt, plus additional to taste

$1/2$ teaspoon freshly ground black pepper, plus additional to taste

$1/2$ teaspoon dried basil

1 teaspoon dried oregano

1 teaspoon sugar

5 sheets phyllo dough

$1/2$ cup melted butter

$1/2$ cup dry bread crumbs

$1/3$ cup freshly shaved Parmigiano-Reggiano cheese

In a 10-inch sauté pan, melt the butter. Add the mushrooms and sauté for 2 to 3 minutes on each side, until they lose some of their moisture. Remove the mushrooms from the pan and drain them on paper towels. In a 3-quart saucepan, heat the olive oil and sauté the onion until it is translucent, about 3 minutes. Add the tomatoes and seasonings, including the sugar, and simmer, uncovered, stirring frequently, for 20 minutes. Taste the sauce, and add additional salt and pepper if necessary. (At this point, the mushrooms and sauce may be refrigerated for up to 2 days; the sauce can be frozen for up to 2 months.)

Preheat the oven to 400° F. Remove the phyllo from the package, and lay it on a counter, covered with a kitchen towel. Remove 1 sheet of phyllo and place it on a cookie sheet lined with parchment or aluminum foil. Brush it with melted butter and sprinkle it with some of the bread crumbs. Repeat this procedure until you have 5 layers of phyllo buttered and sprinkled. Place the mushrooms in the center of the phyllo, making an 8-inch circle. Spoon 1 cup of the sauce over the mushrooms, and top it with the shaved Parmigiano-Reggiano cheese. (Use a swivel vegetable peeler to shave the cheese.) Bring the 4 corners of the phyllo into the center of the pie, and twist them into a knot. (At this point, the pie may be refrigerated overnight or frozen for up to 1 month. If the pie is frozen, wrap it in a jumbo Ziploc-type bag and defrost it in the refrigerator overnight before baking.)

Butter the phyllo, and place it in the preheated oven for 20 to 25 minutes, until the pie is golden brown. Allow the pie to rest 5 minutes before cutting it into wedges for serving.

Serves 6

Potato Florentine Pie

*M*y husband described this pie as comfort food with style. Potatoes are mashed with white Cheddar cheese and cream, topped with a sauté of spinach, and baked golden brown. The potatoes become souffle-like in the oven, and the spinach adds a gorgeous color and taste. Feel free to try different cheeses in the potatoes: Swiss, dry Monterey Jack, or Parmesan.

4 medium russet potatoes

2^1/$_2$ teaspoons salt

3 tablespoons butter

^{1}/$_2$ to ^{3}/$_4$ cup heavy cream

1 cup freshly grated white Cheddar cheese

^{3}/$_4$ teaspoon freshly ground black pepper

^{1}/$_2$ cup finely chopped onion

6 cups fresh spinach, washed and spun dry

^{1}/$_8$ teaspoon freshly grated nutmeg

Preheat the oven to 350° F. Grease a 10-inch round and 2^1/$_2$-inch deep oven-proof casserole dish.

Place the potatoes and 1 teaspoon of salt in a saucepan with water to cover and boil for 15 to 20 minutes, until they are tender when pierced with a sharp knife. Drain the potatoes in a colander and return them to the pan, shaking them over the heat to dry them. Add 2 tablespoons of the butter, ^{1}/$_2$ cup of the cream, and the cheese, and mash the potatoes until they are smooth. (If you prefer lumpy potatoes, go for it!) If the potatoes seem too stiff, add more cream, beating it in a few tablespoons at a time. Season with 1 teaspoon of salt and ^{1}/$_2$ teaspoon of the pepper. Spread the potatoes in the prepared pan and set them aside.

In a 12-inch sauté pan, melt the remaining 1 tablespoon of butter. Add the onion, and sauté until it's limp, about 4 minutes. Add the spinach and toss it with the onion until the spinach begins to wilt. Season the spinach with ¹/₂ teaspoon of salt, ¹/₄ teaspoon of pepper, and the nutmeg. Spread the spinach mixture over the potatoes, leaving a 1-inch border around the outside. Bake the pie for 30 minutes, until puffed and golden. Serve immediately.

Serves 6 to 8

Roasted Tomato Pie with Spinach Pesto Crust

*T*his pie is best made with vine-ripened tomatoes. The tomatoes are roasted with a garlicky oil, then covered with a spicy spinach pesto made with ricotta cheese. The pesto puffs to a golden brown in the oven and makes an impressive statement at the dinner table. If your garden runneth over with tomatoes, try substituting yellow tomatoes.

TOMATO FILLING
5 tablespoons extra virgin olive oil

10 vine-ripened plum or Roma tomatoes (about 1½ pounds)

3 cloves garlic, minced

1 teaspoon chopped fresh oregano, or ½ teaspoon dried

3 leaves fresh basil, chopped, or ½ teaspoon dried

1½ teaspoons salt

½ teaspoon freshly ground black pepper

1 recipe Spinach Pesto Crust (see below)

Preheat the oven to 450° F. Brush a 13 by 9-inch ovenproof baking dish with 1 tablespoon of the olive oil. Slice the tomatoes in half and lay them cut side down, in the baking dish.

In a small mixing bowl, combine the remaining oil with the garlic, oregano, basil, salt, and pepper. Distribute the oil mixture evenly over the tomatoes. Roast the tomatoes for 15 minutes, until the edges are charred, and the tomatoes are softened. Remove the baking dish from the oven and reduce the heat to 375°. While the tomatoes are roasting, prepare the spinach pesto crust.

Spread the pesto over the tomatoes and bake for 20 to 25 minutes, until the crust is set and golden. Remove the pie from the oven and let it stand for 5 minutes before serving.

Spinach Pesto Crust

1 large bunch or 1 (10-ounce) bag fresh spinach, stems discarded, leaves washed and
thoroughly dried

$^1/_2$ teaspoon salt

2 large cloves garlic

1 cup pine nuts

$^1/_2$ cup freshly grated Parmesan cheese

1 cup ricotta cheese

1 egg

In a food processor, combine the spinach, salt, garlic, and pine nuts and pulse
on and off to chop the spinach and garlic. Add the cheeses and egg, processing
until the mixture is smooth.

Serves 6 to 8

Southwestern Vegetable Pie with Tortilla Crust

A light supper or brunch dish, this easy pie goes together quickly and can be refrigerated overnight before baking. Serve it with the avocado black bean salsa, and your guests will be saying "Ole!"

2 tablespoons butter

1 cup finely chopped onion

$^1/_2$ cup seeded and finely chopped Anaheim chile peppers

1 cup finely chopped red bell pepper

1$^1/_2$ cups fresh, or frozen and defrosted corn kernels

6 eggs

1$^1/_2$ cups milk

1 teaspoon salt

$^1/_2$ teaspoon freshly ground black pepper

$^1/_4$ teaspoon cayenne

4 tablespoons chopped fresh cilantro

12 (6-inch) corn tortillas, torn into 1-inch pieces

3 cups freshly grated Monterey Jack cheese (or a combination of your favorites)

1 recipe Avocado Black Bean Salsa (see below)

Spray a 13 by 9-inch ovenproof baking dish with a non-stick cooking spray. In a sauté pan, melt the butter. Add the onion and peppers, and sauté for 3 to 4 minutes. Add the corn and stir to blend. Remove the pan from the heat and set it aside.

In a mixing bowl, whisk together the eggs, milk, salt, pepper, cayenne, and cilantro. Spread one third of the tortillas in the bottom of the casserole dish. Top with half the pepper and corn mixture, a third of the cheese, and half of the egg mixture. Spread another layer of tortillas over the egg mixture, saving the last third for the top. Sprinkle the tortillas with what is left of the pepper mixture, more cheese (saving half for the top), and the rest of the eggs. Top this layer with the remaining tortillas and sprinkle the top with cheese. Refrigerate the pie for at least 4 hours, or up to 24 hours. Make the salsa.

When ready to bake, preheat the oven to 350° F. Allow the casserole to sit at room temperature for 30 minutes, then bake it for 35 to 45 minutes, until the pie is puffed and golden. Remove it from the oven and let it stand for 10 minutes before cutting and serving, accompanied by the avocado black bean salsa. (If you would like to make this pie with chicken or shrimp, layer the cooked chicken or shrimp with the corn-pepper mixture, and bake as directed.)

Avocado Black Bean Salsa

1 Haas avocado, peeled and cut into $1/2$-inch dice

$1/4$ cup chopped red onion

$1/4$ cup chopped Anaheim chile pepper

2 tablespoons chopped fresh cilantro

$1/2$ cup peeled, seeded, and chopped fresh tomato

1 cup cooked black beans

2 tablespoons freshly squeezed lime juice

$1/2$ teaspoon salt

6 shakes Tabasco sauce

$1/4$ teaspoon freshly ground black pepper

In a glass mixing bowl, combine all the ingredients and stir to blend. Refrigerate until ready to serve.

Serves 6 to 8

Spinach, Artichoke, and Feta Pie

*T*his deliciously easy free-form pie is the perfect dish for a casual dinner with friends. The pie can be made two days ahead of time and refrigerated, or frozen for up to 2 months. Paired with a field green and pear salad, it can turn your dinner table into an elegant bistro—just add candles and your favorite wine.

1 pound fresh spinach, washed and trimmed of tough stems
2 quarts boiling water
2 (4-ounce) jars marinated artichokes, drained and chopped
4 ounces feta cheese
$1/3$ cup freshly grated Parmesan cheese
2 eggs
$1/4$ teaspoon freshly ground black pepper
Pinch of grated nutmeg
5 sheets phyllo dough
$1/2$ cup melted butter
$1/2$ cup dry bread crumbs

Place the spinach in a colander in the sink and pour the boiling water over it. Drain the spinach, and chop it coarsely. Place the spinach, artichokes, feta, Parmesan, and eggs in a large mixing bowl and stir to combine. Add the pepper and nutmeg, stirring again. (The filling can be kept refrigerated for up to 2 days before forming the pie.)

Unwrap the phyllo and place it on a clean counter covered with a clean kitchen towel. Place 1 sheet of phyllo on a baking sheet lined with aluminum foil or parchment paper. Brush the phyllo with melted butter and sprinkle it with some of the bread crumbs. Repeat until you have 5 layers of phyllo buttered and crumbed. Place the spinach mixture in the center and form it into an 8-inch circle, pressing the filling so that it is the same thickness all the way around the circle. Bring the corners of the phyllo into the center twist them into a knot. (The pie can be refrigerated for up to 2 days before baking, or frozen for up to 2 months. Defrost the pie overnight in the refrigerator before baking.)

When ready to bake, preheat the oven to 400° F. Brush the phyllo with additional melted butter and bake the pie for 20 minutes, or until the top is golden brown.

Serves 6

Swiss Chard Pie with Bruschetta Crust

A gorgeous combination of vivid green Swiss chard, topped with a red tomato bruschetta crust, this has all the attributes of a perfect pie. Swiss chard has tough stems, which can also be used, but they require longer cooking, so I have not used them here. If you would like to use them, boil them first in the water until just tender, then add the leaves.

CHARD FILLING

3 bunches Swiss chard (stems removed) washed, drained, and cut into 2-inch pieces

8 quarts boiling salted water

1/4 cup extra virgin olive oil

2 cloves garlic

1 teaspoon salt, or more to taste

1/2 teaspoon freshly ground black pepper, or more to taste

BRUSCHETTA CRUST

1 loaf French bread, cut into 3/4-inch-thick slices, toasted on both sides

2 cups 1/2-inch diced ripe tomatoes

2 cloves garlic, minced

1/4 cup chopped fresh basil

1/4 cup plus 2 tablespoons extra virgin olive oil

1/2 teaspoon salt

1/4 teaspoon freshly ground black pepper

1/4 cup freshly grated Pecorino Romano cheese

For the filling, drop the chard into the pot of boiling water, and cook it for 3 minutes, or until the leaves are tender. Drain the chard. In a large sauté pan, heat the oil, add the garlic, and sauté until it becomes golden. Add the chard to the pan, tossing it with the oil, salt, and pepper. Taste, and correct the seasoning if necessary. Remove the garlic cloves and spread the chard in a 12-inch round ovenproof pan.

For the crust, preheat the broiler for 10 minutes. Top the chard with the toasted bread. In a glass mixing bowl, combine the tomatoes, garlic, basil, olive oil, salt, and pepper. Stir to combine. Top each bread slice with 1 to 2 table-spoons of the tomato mixture. Sprinkle the tops of the bruschetta with cheese. Run the pie under the broiler until the cheese begins to bubble, about 3–5 minutes. Serve immediately.

Serves 6 to 8

Wild Rice Pie with Blue Cheese Onion Crust

*T*his dish is so simple, yet elegant enough for a special occasion. A blend of white and wild rice is cooked under a crust of caramelized onions and tangy blue cheese. If you can find Maytag blue cheese, its mellow flavor is best for this dish. The rice and onions can be cooked ahead of time, and the dish can be finished in the oven just before serving.

WILD RICE PIE

$^1/_2$ cup wild rice

$3^1/_2$ cups vegetable broth

$1^1/_2$ teaspoons salt

$^1/_2$ teaspoon freshly ground black pepper

2 tablespoons butter

$^1/_2$ cup finely chopped carrot

$^1/_4$ cup finely chopped celery

1 teaspoon dried marjoram

$^1/_2$ teaspoon dried thyme

1 cup long-grain white rice

1 recipe Onion Crust (see below)

$^1/_2$ cup crumbled Maytag blue cheese, or more to taste

Wash the wild rice in water. In a 3-quart saucepan, bring $1^1/_2$ cups of the broth to a boil. Add the wild rice, 1 teaspoon of the salt, and $^1/_4$ teaspoon of pepper, and simmer, covered, for 15 minutes. In a small sauté pan, melt the butter, add the carrot, celery, marjoram, and thyme, and sauté for 2 minutes. Add the long-grain rice, tossing to coat the grains well. Add the white rice mixture to the wild rice along with the remaining vegetable broth, salt, and pepper. Simmer, covered, for an additional 15 to 20 minutes, until the rice is tender and the liquid is absorbed. Spray an ovenproof baking dish with non-stick cooking spray.

Remove the rice from the saucepan, and spread it in the bottom of the baking dish. Cover and refrigerate until ready to bake. Preheat the oven to 400° F. Spread the onions over the rice mixture. Sprinkle the onions with the blue cheese and bake for 10 minutes, until the cheese is melted. Cut into wedges or squares and serve immediately.

Onion Crust

4 tablespoons butter

6 large onions, sliced $1/4$ inch thick

$1/2$ teaspoon salt

$1/4$ teaspoon freshly ground black pepper

1 teaspoon sugar

In a large sauté pan, melt the butter. Add the onions, salt, and pepper, and sauté over medium-high heat until the onions begin to soften, about 3–4 minutes. Stir the onions constantly, so that they do not burn. After 5 minutes, when the onions begin to wilt, sprinkle them with the sugar, turn the heat up a bit, and sauté until the onions begin to caramelize and turn a deep golden brown. (At this point the onions may be refrigerated until ready to bake.)

Serves 6 to 8

Zucchini Pie with Parmesan Rice Crust

*T*his is a great dish to make when your garden is overflowing with baseball-bat-sized zucchini. Grate the zucchini in the summer and freeze it in 16-ounce Ziploc bags to make this great pie in winter. Leftover pie is wonderful for breakfast!

3 tablespoons butter

$1/2$ cup finely chopped onion

2 cloves garlic, minced

4 cups grated zucchini (about $2^1/2$ pounds)

$1^1/2$ teaspoons salt

$1/2$ teaspoon freshly ground black pepper

4 shakes Tabasco sauce

2 tablespoons all-purpose flour

$1^1/2$ cups vegetable broth

1 cup heavy cream

$3/4$ cup long-grain white rice

$3/4$ cup freshly grated Parmesan cheese

Preheat the oven to 400° F. Spray a 13 by 9-inch ovenproof baking dish with non-stick cooking spray.

In a sauté pan, melt the butter, add the onion and garlic, and cook, stirring, until the onion is softened, about 2–3 minutes. Add the zucchini, and cook until the zucchini is no longer giving off moisture, about 4–6 minutes. Season with salt, pepper, and Tabasco. Sprinkle with the flour and cook, whisking, for 2 minutes. Gradually stir in the broth, whisking until smooth. Add the cream, and bring to a boil.

Pour the zucchini mixture into the casserole dish. Sprinkle with the rice and then the cheese. Bake for 25 to 35 minutes, until the rice is tender and the cheese is golden.

Serves 8

Source
Guide

Source Guide

IF YOU live in an area with limited availability for certain ingredients, here are a few sources you can contact to obtain their products.

Boyajian, Inc.
385 California Street
Newton, MA 02160
617 527-6677
Flavored oils, smoked salmon, caviar.

The Green House
P.O. Box 231069
Encinitas, CA 92023
619 942-5371
Dehydrated herbs.

Cabot Creamery
P.O. Box 128
Cabot, VT 05647
Visitor's Center: 1-800-837-4261
Mail order: 1-800-639-3198
Web Site: *www.cabotcheese.com*
Absolutely the best white cheddar cheese in the world, plus butter, cream cheese, and other cheeses.

King Arthur Flour
P.O. Box 876
Norwich, VT 05055
800 777-4434
Web Site: *http://home.kingarthurflour.com*
Baking equipment, exceptional flours and grains, spices, oils, and unusual ingredients. (Even Day-Glo cheese powder for macaroni and cheese!)

Frieda's Inc.
4465 Corporate Center Drive
Los Alamitos, CA 90720
714 826-6100
Web Site: *http://www.friedas.com*
Purveyors of unusual food stuffs, notably vegetables and fruits.

Pepperidge Farm, Inc.
Norwalk, CT 06856
800 762-8301
Web Site: *http://www.puffpastry.com*
Frozen puff pastry dough and phyllo.

SAF Instant Yeast
400 South Fourth Street
Suite 310
Minneapolis, MN 55415
800 641-4651
Absolutely the best yeast on the market.

Superior Quality Foods
P.O. Box 646
Claremont, CA 91711
800 429-FOOD
Better than bouillon products—including lobster stock, beef, chicken, clam, and vegetable.

Williams-Sonoma
P.O. Box 7456
San Francisco, CA 94120
800 541-2233
An incredible catalogue and stores with just about anything you could want or need to make anything edible.

Index

Index